Catholic Spirituality
From A to Z

Catholic Spirituality From A to Z

An Inspirational Dictionary

SUSAN MUTO

SERVANT PUBLICATIONS
ANN ARBOR, MICHIGAN

Other Books by Susan Muto

Approaching the Sacred: An Introduction to Spiritual Reading
Blessings That Make Us Be: A Formative Approach to Living the Beatitudes
Caring for the Caregiver
Celebrating the Single Life
Dear Master: Letters on Spiritual Direction Inspired by Saint John of the Cross
John of the Cross for Today: The Ascent
John of the Cross for Today: The Dark Night
The Journey Homeward
Late Have I Loved Thee: The Recovery of Intimacy
Meditation in Motion
Pathways of Spiritual Living
A Practical Guide to Spiritual Reading
Renewed at Each Awakening
Steps Along the Way
Womanspirit: Reclaiming the Deep Feminine in our Human Spirituality
Words of Wisdom for Our World: The Precautions and Counsels of St. John of the Cross

With Adrian van Kaam

Aging Gracefully
Am I Living a Spiritual Life?
The Commandments: Ten Ways to a Happy Life and a Healthy Soul
Commitment: Key to Christian Maturity
Divine Guidance: Seeking to Find and Follow the Will of God
The Emergent Self
Epiphany Manual on the Art and Discipline of Formation-in-Common
Formation Guide to Becoming Spiritually Mature
Harnessing Stress: A Spiritual Quest
Healthy and Holy Under Stress: A Royal Road to Wise Living
The Participant Self
The Power of Appreciation: A New Approach to Personal and Relational Healing
Practicing the Prayer of Presence
Songs for Every Season
Stress and the Search for Happiness: A New Challenge for Christian Spirituality

Charis Books is an imprint of Servant Publications especially designed to serve Roman Catholics.

Nihil Obstat: November 30, 1999, by Joseph J. Kleppner, S.T.L., Ph.D., Censor Liborum
Imprimatur: December 2, 1999, by Most Reverend Donald Wuerl, Bishop of Pittsburgh
The Nihil Obstat and the Imprimatur are declarations that this work is considered to be free from doctrinal or moral error. It is not implied that those who have granted the same agree with the contents, opinions, or statements expressed.

Servant Publications
P.O. Box 8617
Ann Arbor, MI 48107

Cover design: Paz Design Group, Salem, Oregon
Cover illustration: Saint Matthew, Evangelist Angel by Giusto di Giovanni Menabuoi. Bapistry of the Cathedral, Padua, Italy/Superstock.

00 01 02 03 10 9 8 7 6 5 4 3 2 1

Printed in the United States of America
ISBN 1-56955-160-X

LIBRARY OF CONGRESS CATALOGING-IN-PUBLICATION DATA

Muto, Susan Annette.
Catholic spirituality from A to Z : an inspirational dictionary / Susan Muto.
p. cm.
Includes bibliographical references (p.) and index.
ISBN 1-56955-160-X
1. Spirituality—Catholic Church—Dictionaries. 2. Catholic Church—Doctrines—Dictionaries. I. Title.

BX2350.65.M88 2000
248'.03—dc21 00-031570

Contents

Introduction 9
A 11
B 23
C 33
D 59
E 73
F 79
G 87
H 95
I 99
J 103
K 109
L 113
M 119
N 127
O 131
P 133
Q 143
R 145
S 149
T 161
U 169
V 171
W 177
X 181
Y 183
Z 185
Index 187
Bibliography 191
About the Author 205

"The [Second Vatican] Council Fathers spoke in the languages of the Gospel, the language of the Sermon on the Mount and the Beatitudes. In the Council's message God is presented *in his absolute lordship over all things,* but also as *the One who ensures the authentic autonomy of earthly realities.*

The best preparation for the new millennium, therefore, can only be expressed in a renewed commitment *to apply,* as faithfully as possible, *the teachings of Vatican II to the life of every individual and of the whole Church.*"

Pope John Paul II,
On the Coming of the Third Millennium, 19–20.

Introduction

This inspirational dictionary taps into the founding sources and fresh streams of our two-thousand-year faith and formation tradition, with its treasury of wisdom for living. However, there is more to mine in this lodestone of riches than this or any dictionary or anthology can hope to exhaust.

This book will explore the lives and teachings of several ancient Fathers and Doctors of the undivided Church, East and West, many pre-Reformation spiritual masters of the medieval Western Christian tradition, and classical authors of the modern period, all of whom seek the depth dimension of union with God. Missing from these pages but not from my heart are the post-Reformation spiritual writers, whose works I also teach. To include all of these would require another dictionary!

In the stream of formation wisdom that flows from the early Church to the present era, we find a record of goodness, truth, and beauty that brings us to our knees in awe and gratitude. Truly the Holy Spirit guides the body of Christ, his Church, "from glory unto glory" (2 Corinthians 3:18). This dictionary is but a pebble in an ocean of grace.

My aim is to complement the wealth of wisdom every user of this text will find in lengthier compilations and especially in the new *Catechism of the Catholic Church,* which has been a source of continual inspiration and guidance to me. In the dictionary I often refer to it simply as the *Catechism.* It offers, in the words of my colleague Father Adrian van Kaam, C.S.Sp., Ph.D., privileged access to the Divine Information of the Revelation.

The choice of concept, tradition, saint and scholar, period, and person is my own and is the result of prayer, appraisal, and years of teaching in the fields of literature and formative spirituality. Consult the *A to Z's* whenever you need them to clarify something you do not fully understand, to learn about the great "cloud of witnesses" (Hebrews 12:1), or to increase your knowledge of our Church's teaching and traditions. Names, words, and phrases in boldface refer to complementary A to Z's you can review for further information.

I thank my editor at Servant Publications, Bert Ghezzi, for bringing the idea for this book to my attention in the first place and for seeing it through to publication. I am most grateful for the support and suggestions given to me throughout the course of its writing by Father Adrian van Kaam on behalf of our Epiphany Association and its many resources and programs in adult faith formation.

To my staff at Epiphany House, most notably our Administrative Secretary, Mary Lou Perez, and our Business Manager and my expert and always patient typist, Vicki Bittner, I owe a lasting debt of gratitude. To write a dictionary is one thing; to have it so professionally crafted is another.

On a personal note, it is my fondest hope that this easy-to-use dictionary will serve as a catalyst to stimulate your daily reading of Scripture and the writings of the spiritual masters as you reclaim in your own life the classics of Catholic spirituality in both the pre- and post-Reformation eras. Allow each entry to whet your appetite for further study of the Bible and the *Catechism*. Let it instill in you a drive to pursue higher education in the field of spiritual formation. Once this book gets you off the ground in your studies, let the Holy Spirit teach you over a lifetime how to soar!

Abandonment to Divine Providence

Jesus Christ is the best teacher of this virtue essential to spiritual maturity. It is he who said from the cruelty of the Cross, *"Eloi, Eloi, lema sabachthani?"* which means, "My God, my God, why have you forsaken me?" (Mark 15:34). He also said at this darkest hour of human devastation, "Father, into your hands I commend my spirit" (Luke 23:46). Jesus teaches us the way of abandonment in word and deed by surrendering his whole being *to* the mystery of the Father's love-will for his life. Never did he succumb to the temptation to feel abandoned *by* the mystery, nor must we.

Following in Jesus' footsteps means that we, too, must strive with the help of grace to trust without reservation in the ultimate benevolence of the God who first loved us (1 John 4:10). As trust grows, so does the unconditional willingness to place our whole life under the canopy of divine guidance and to conform our decisions and actions to the teaching of Christ and the Church. The more abandoned we are, the less likely we are to deviate from the way of perfection recommended by saints and spiritual masters from biblical times to the present era.

The **French School of Spirituality,** with its teaching on abnegation or self-denial, is an example of the immense ascetical and mystical tradition that has sprung from this virtue. Every occasion Holy Providence allows presents to us another opportunity to depend more completely upon God and to let go of any inclination or habit, action or condition that would turn us away from him. For the abandoned soul, every obstacle can become a formation opportunity.

Acquisition of the Holy Spirit

In his farewell discourse in the Gospel of John (14:15-26), Jesus promises us the Holy Spirit, the Spirit of Truth. He is the Counselor whom the Father will send in Jesus' name to teach us all things and to remind us of everything Jesus said to us. This Spirit, Third Person of the Blessed Trinity, animates all of creation with his life-giving breath, and awakens within us **faith, hope,** and **charity** as well as the power to pray and the courage to make a firm commitment to support the mission of the Church. Especially in the sacrament of **Confirmation** we acquire the **gifts of the Holy Spirit;** as we grow to spiritual maturity the **fruits of the Spirit** ripen and grow within us.

The most foundational forming, reforming, and transforming source of our Christian faith and formation tradition is, therefore, the Holy Spirit. The outpouring of the Spirit by the Risen Christ creates and recreates the Church and its members through the power of grace. The teaching and practice, which the Spirit inspires, constitute the living deposit of wisdom offered to us in accordance with the doctrine of the Church and its expression in word and worship. The Holy Spirit, source of this inspiration and of our understanding of the Revelation, communicates to the Church and her members not only the content and meaning of the faith but also its basic transforming potential: "Now the Lord is the Spirit, and where the Spirit of the Lord is, there is freedom. All of us, gazing with unveiled face on the glory of the Lord, are being transformed into the same image from glory to glory, as from the Lord who is the Spirit" (2 Corinthians 3:17-18).

Aelred of Rievaulx, Saint

(1109-67) Aelred, a man of noble ancestry, spent his early years mingling with members of the Scottish court, but worldly success and popularity could not satisfy his restless heart. He became a **Cistercian** monk, entering the Rievaulx Abbey in England in 1134. Aelred lived in the "Golden Age" of the Cistercian reform, during which there were at least five hundred foundations of the order in Europe alone, thanks to the incredible inspiration and leadership of **Saint Bernard of Clairvaux.** Aelred was an excellent orator and a wise and holy man; his gentle yet firm leadership style attracted over six hundred monks to his abbey.

From his earliest days in the monastery, Aelred embraced *The Rule of Saint Benedict* and found in it the key to monastic life: **contemplation** or resting in God. He regarded contemplation to be the ground of Christian **charity,** the wellspring of **spiritual friendship,** and the source of social action. Unlike some of his day, Aelred viewed the inclusive style of spiritual friendship as the fruit of charity.

Ambrose, Saint

(c. 340-97) Ambrose, an aristocrat by birth, chose to follow in his father's footsteps and pursue a career in public office as a servant of the Roman Empire. By 370, he had attained by worldly standards a position of some prominence, having become provincial governor of two provinces in the north of Italy with headquarters in Milan. But Divine Providence had other plans for Ambrose. When the bishop of Milan died in 374, Ambrose found himself embroiled in a bitter dispute between two factions, Catholic and Arian, over whom to choose as his successor. (See **Arianism**.)

Though only a catechumen, Ambrose was to his immense surprise lifted up by the people as the only acceptable candidate for this holy office. He ultimately accepted this commission as God's will, and within a week was baptized, confirmed, ordained, and consecrated bishop of Milan, a man already loved by civil leaders and laity for his affable disposition, his sense of **justice,** his administrative skills and scholarship, and, most of all, for his remarkable gifts as a preacher and teacher of the **faith**. His first act was to give away his worldly possessions and to embrace the cross with all its austere beauty.

As one of the greatest Latin Doctors of the Church and as an exemplary shepherd of his flock, Ambrose sought to gain complete victory over the Arian heresy. Ambrose's sermons on the six days of creation (*Hexameron*) are regarded as a literary and Christian masterpiece, containing some surprisingly contemporary observations on human nature and our pre-existing, pre-formed relationship to our Creator.

As knowledgeable a theologian and philosopher as he was, Ambrose was also a Roman poet and a composer of hymns. He never lost his gift for eloquence of speech, but, as he showed his people, neither preaching without practice nor practice without prayer can bear lasting fruit. This good and faithful servant of the servants of God journeyed to his final homeland on Good Friday, April 4, 397. To the end, he suffered with Christ so that through Christ he might share abundantly in his consolation (cf. 2 Corinthians 1:5).

Angelic Orders

In our faith tradition, there are nine designations for these heavenly beings: Thrones, Cherubim, Seraphim, Dominions, Powers, Authorities, Principalities, Archangels, and Angels. *Thrones* remain always and forever in the presence of the Most High, enjoying transcendence over every earthly defect. *Cherubim* receive the greatest gifts of God's light and the beneficial outpouring of his wisdom. *Seraphim* are carriers of the warmth of God's love, whose fire casts aside the shadows that obscure his goodness. These orders together commune with God and share in his work, imitating insofar as possible the beauty of his **contemplation** and the generosity of his activity, proclaiming in one voice, "Holy, holy, holy is the LORD of hosts! ... All the earth is filled with his glory!" (Isaiah 6:3; cf. Revelation 4:8).

The angels of middle rank reveal,

Angels

Indeed the Word of God teaches us that the Law was given to us by the angels. Before the days of the Law and after it had come, it was the angels who uplifted our illustrious ancestors toward the divine and they did so by prescribing roles of conduct, by turning them from wandering and sin to the right way of truth, or by coming to announce and explain sacred orders, hidden visions, or transcendent mysteries, or divine prophecies.

–Pseudo-Dionysius

according to **Pseudo-Dionysius,** three distinct qualities. *Dominions* exercise not domination but the true source of all dominion: benevolence. *Powers* show us the courage that overcomes cowardice. *Authorities* again do not exercise any tyranny over others but uplift them toward the things of God. All together these orders create harmony in the universe and manifest perfect conformity to God.

The final rank in the celestial hierarchy begins with the *Principalities,* who make known the principles of order and procession, establishing boundaries and guarding us from wandering off to worship false gods. The *archangels* help us to trust totally in the providence of God and to follow his directives with docility. As for the *angels,* they bring the word of God, his glad tidings, to hearts open to receive these inspirations and to live by their light. (See also **Guardian Angels**.)

Anselm of Canterbury, Saint

(c. 1033-1109) Saint Anselm, a philosopher, theologian, and spiritual master, wrote *Prayers and Meditations,* one of the most influential books in medieval spirituality, a text read by monks and laity alike. He wrote it after he entered the Benedictine Abbey of Bec in Normandy in 1059. In it he writes: "I do not seek to understand so that I may believe, but I believe so that I may understand."

For Anselm, to desire God was to seek him; to find him was to love him. He used this poetic style of composition to arouse his own and others' hearts to **compunction,** detestation of sin, and confidence in the **mercy** of God. His aim was "to stir up the mind of the reader ... to self-examination." This was for him not a matter of discursive analysis but an invitation to enter the inner chamber of the soul, to quiet all distractions, and to enjoy being present to the Lord. In this way the work of the analytical intelligence would not interfere with the higher reason illumined by **faith**. Anselm modeled for his fellow monks that the will to love and the obligation to serve are inseparable. He fulfilled this divine directive in such a remarkable way that over a thirty-year period this benevolent and brilliant monk earned the title "Father of Scholasticism."

In 1093, despite the fact that he wanted to continue in his office as abbot of Bec, he was named archbishop of Canterbury in England. From that time until his death, his public life denied him the peace he craved. He found himself caught up in dissensions over the relations between church and state, between ecclesial independence and political control, first under King William II and then under Henry I. On at least two occasions, Anselm had to retreat to Rome when efforts to oust him as archbishop became too heated. All was not lost, however. While in exile, he wrote one of his best-known works on atonement and the Incarnation, *Cur Deus Homo* [Why God Became Man]. That sin's inexorable offense could only be expiated by Jesus' total self-gift became for Anselm the surest proof of the lengths to which divine love would go to save us.

Antony of Egypt, Saint

(c. 251-356) This exemplary Desert Father, sometimes called "Antony the Abbot," set the standard for monasticism in the West, thanks in great measure to **Saint Athanasius of Alexandria**'s firsthand account of his life. Antony came from a wealthy family living in Egypt. He might have followed in his parents' footsteps had he not undergone a conversion experience so powerful it changed his life from its worldly beginnings to its otherworldly ends.

After the death of his parents, according to the account of his biographer, Antony "went to the Lord's house as usual and gathering his thoughts, he considered how the apostles, forsaking everything, followed the Savior, and how in Acts some sold what they possessed and took the proceeds and placed them at the feet of the apostles...." While he was in church pondering these things, Antony heard the Gospel being read. What the Lord said to the rich man pierced his heart: "If you seek perfection, go, sell your possessions, and give to the poor. You will then have treasure in heaven" (Matthew 19:21).

Antony knew this reading was not a coincidence but a direct act of Divine Providence. Without hesitation he went out from the Lord's house and did exactly what the Scriptures advised. He sold or gave away his property to family members and the poor, and submitted himself as a disciple to a hermit living nearby. Around 273, he finally heeded the deeper call beckoning him to **solitude** and strict **asceticism**. He chose the desert around the Nile Valley, where he stayed for the next twenty years.

From 306 onward, he accepted disciples and founded a monastery in the hermitical style he preferred. On a few occasions he had no choice but to leave his beloved solitude and respond to a call to go to Alexandria to join Athanasius' campaign against the Arians and to support Christians being persecuted there. Always he returned to his beloved cell, for in the city he described himself as a fish out of water. In many ways he was the precursor of the **Benedictine** spirit of work and prayer, lived always with moderation and compassion. It was Antony's firm belief that "if we stretch the brethren beyond measure they will soon break." Only when Antony learned what the desert had to teach him could he risk being a teacher of others, a model of **charity**, a healer of soul and body. He lived to be 105, enjoying relatively good health and continual vigilance of heart.

Apparitions

"Appearances" refer in the strict sense to either a vision or a bodily manifestation permitted by God and ideally approved of by the Church, as are the apparitions of the **Blessed Virgin Mary**, for example, at Lourdes, Fatima, and Guadalupe. Apparitions are not uncommon in Scripture and are often disclosed through the mediation of God's messengers, the **angels**. Authentic apparitions evoke awe, are often marked by an increase in **faith**, **hope**, and **charity**, and may be accompanied by miracles.

To guard against hysteria and "psychic contagion," such extraordinary phenomena must be submitted to the most careful scrutiny of the Church, tested over time and in keeping with the strictest theological and mystical standards. Often apparitions, especially of the Blessed Mother, yield images or statues that evoke veneration. The *Catechism of the Catholic Church* says that such veneration is not at all a form of idolatry, since "the honor rendered to an image passes to its prototype" [2132] or to the person portrayed in it, for example, Our Lady of Lourdes. The honor paid to her image or apparition in no way lessens or replaces the adoration due to God alone.

To the degree that any appearance moves us from its visible manifestation to its invisible reality, it can be an epiphany in our lives, evoking affection and joy. The awe we feel is not directed toward the apparition as such but toward the person or spirit it represents and the living mystery of faith its presence evokes.

Arianism

Arius (256-326), a priest of Alexandria, taught that Christ, though more perfect than other creatures, was still a part of creation and was neither the equal of the Father nor true God. This teaching created a faction within the Church and was refuted by many Church Fathers of that era including **Saint Ambrose** (*Hexameron*) and **Saint Athanasius** (*Orations Against the Arians* and *On the Incarnation*). The heresy was officially condemned by the Council of Nicea in 325, which upheld the traditional belief in the "consubstantial" identity of Father and Son, expressed so beautifully in the Nicene Creed wherein we pray, "We believe in one Lord, Jesus Christ, the only Son of God, eternally begotten of the Father, God from God, Light from Light, true God from true God, begotten, not made, one in Being with the Father."

Aridity

This state of spiritual dryness has been compared by writers in the ascetical-mystical tradition to the **desert experience** or the **dark night of the soul**. A person faithful in prayer who has already experienced a spiritual awakening or the sensation of **consolation** may experience a sense of **desolation** until the aridity subsides. **Saint John of the Cross** writes of this arid feeling at the beginning of *The Spiritual Canticle,* asking, "Where have you hidden, Beloved, and left me moaning.... I went out calling you and you were gone." Not surprisingly, he sees this state as a meritorious step on the way to spiritual maturity. He even calls aridity "a sublime path to dark contemplation" in his book *The Ascent of Mount Carmel,* and differentiates this state from mere melancholy, depression, or temperament. Experience tells him that this can be a time of profound spiritual deepening. After all, as Saint John reminds us, it was at the point of utmost aridity, when Jesus felt abandoned by everyone and when he was reduced to nothing, that he accomplished the awesome feat of our salvation.

The positive effect of aridity is that it makes spirituality not a matter of feeling but of willing, not a question of the emotions but of **faith**. It is a sign that the soul is moving from sensible sweetness to mature rest in God. The danger inherent in this same state is that one might be tempted to abandon prayer. In her autobiography, **Saint Teresa of Avila** says that she could not pray for almost eighteen years without the help of a book, so dry did she feel. However, Saint Teresa also saw that when the soil in which grace grows becomes dry, it is easier to pull up the weeds of inordinate attachments. Then one is more ready to receive the rain of comfort when it comes—not with a thunderbolt but with a gentle, quiet breeze.

Ascetical Practices

Ascetical practices are spiritual disciplines intended to aid our growth in spiritual maturity. (See **Asceticism.**) These disciplines include both interior and external practices.

Controlling one's thoughts, one example of an interior discipline, is an ascetical practice as old as the desert tradition. **Evagrius Ponticus,** in describing his own ascetical experiences, lists the eight evil thoughts (sometimes called "capital" or "deadly" sins) we need to eliminate if we want to become true followers of Christ: gluttony, lust, avarice, *acedia* (sloth or melancholy), anger, boredom, vainglory, and pride. Such thoughts pose major obstacles to prayer and direct communication with God, which is the essence of the mystical life.

External ascetical practices may include praying at set times, fasting, and abstaining from certain foods and other bodily mortifications, provided one avoids excess in any form through moderation. For example, even though **Saint Thérèse of Lisieux** wanted to be a missionary in China, the ascesis of her weak, consumptive physical condition required that she stay in her convent, eat as well as possible, and get plenty of rest, especially toward the end of her young life. Her ascesis became the little way of **spiritual childhood**, where she utilized the smallest mortification, like smiling at a sister for whom she felt little or no natural affinity, to bring her closer to the love of Jesus.

If we would be disciples of Christ, we must be willing to discipline ourselves in the way his grace directs us—not out of tune but in tune with our limits and possibilities. That is why the Letter to the Hebrews assures us, "At the time, all discipline seems a cause not for joy but for pain, yet later it brings the peaceful fruit of righteousness to those who are trained by it" (Hebrews 12:11). Thus strengthened, we can run "the race that lies before us while keeping our eyes fixed on Jesus, the leader and perfecter of faith" (Hebrews 12:1-2).

The difference between the ascetic life, in which human action predominates, and the mystical life, in which God's action takes the initiative, might be illustrated by the difference between rowing a boat and sailing it. The motion of the oar might be compared with ascetic effort, while the sail suggests mystical receptivity unfurled to catch the wind of the Spirit.

Asceticism

From the Greek *askein* or *askesis*, this word means "to exercise" or "to train." Hence an "ascetic" is one who practices self-discipline, self-denial, **solitude, detachment**, prayer, **poverty**, and charitable works as conditions to enhance his or her graced union with God. Asceticism is not an end in itself but a means toward living a life that is committed physically, mentally, emotionally, morally, and spiritually to the pursuit of holiness. Ascetics (all who wish to remain faithful to their baptismal promises and to resist temptation) must come, therefore, to a high degree of self-knowledge.

The main aim of asceticism is to break through the illusion that anyone or anything but God can fulfill our longing for happiness. Whatever comes close to doing so is but a pointer to what is beyond, a means toward our goal, not an end in itself or a project of self-salvation.

It has been said by many saints that the ascetical life is the only reliable basis on which to build a mystical life since we can never redeem ourselves or merit the saving graces God so liberally bestows. In other words, asceticism is to **mysticism** what self-control is to Christian perfection. One without the other may be suspect. Obeying God's law is good and essential, but of itself it cannot save us. Without love our spiritual life is dead, even though we may boast of our moral uprightness.

Neither is asceticism a streamlined approach that entails the same practices for everyone. As the *Catechism* reminds us, it must be "adapted to the situations that confront" us, and always done in a spirit of "obedience to God's commandments, exercise of the moral virtues, and fidelity to prayer" [2340].

Athanasius of Alexandria, Saint

(295-373) Bishop and Doctor of the Church, Saint Athanasius was a staunch defender against the heresy of **Arianism.** So bitter was his fight against the Arians that Athanasius had to suffer exile four times before the people rose up in his defense, compelling the very Synods that had held him suspect to cease interfering with his theological and pastoral pursuit of the truth. The legacy of his life can be found not only in his various discourses and defenses but also in his biography of **Saint Antony of Egypt**.

Augustine of Hippo, Saint

(354-430) Augustine is one of the most influential and prolific of the Fathers and Doctors of Western Christendom, due in great measure to his classical works, *The Confessions, The City of God,* and *On the Trinity,* and his sermons on Genesis, Psalms, and the Gospels. Though baptized Catholic, Augustine was as famous a sinner before his **conversion** as he was a saint, bishop, and defender of the **faith** afterward.

He writes of this *metanoia* in his

Confessions, of that day in the garden in 387, when his admission of sin gave way to his longing for forgiveness and he read, as if for the first time, Romans 13:13-14, after which he said, "No further wished I to read, nor was there need to do so. Instantly, in truth, at the end of this sentence, as if before a peaceful light streaming into my heart, all the dark shadows of doubt fled away."

Augustine was the first to admit that without the prayers of his mother, Saint Monica (c. 331-87), who nurtured his faith despite his resistance, he might never have been able to escape the "hissing cauldron of lust" and the pride of the intellect that for so long had held him in bondage. Happily for Augustine, the Holy Spirit used the sermons of **Saint Ambrose**, bishop of Milan, to break the chains that bound his heart and to turn him toward orthodoxy.

Once caught by grace, Augustine never let go. His "passion for the wisdom of eternal truth" was at long last satisfied. Ordained a priest in 391, he became by 395 bishop of Hippo in northern Africa, an office he held for thirty-five years. He also established a religious community and composed the Augustinian rule as the source of its governance and inspiration. He lived a modest life as companion to his brothers and friend of the poor, while using his writing skills to shore up a Church shaken by the very heresies he once espoused, Gnosticism and Manichaeanism. He did his utmost to preserve Christian doctrine in the face of barbarian invasions, the collapse of the Roman Empire, and the Dark Ages that were to descend upon the Church.

Perhaps in overreaction to his own materialistic life, Augustine appeared in some of his teachings to condemn bodily pleasure for any reason other than procreation, but with the passage of history scholars have been able to sift the chaff of time-bound accretions from the wheat of foundational truths, rendering Augustine one of the greatest influences on the formulations of Church doctrine and the theology of love. In fact, the cultivation of **charity** was for him the goal of the common life.

Augustine died at the age of seventy-six, as the Vandals invaded his episcopal city. What this "Doctor of Grace" once knew by intuition, he then knew by experience. In what may be the most quoted phrase from his *Confessions*, he proclaims with full confidence: "You are great, O Lord, and greatly to be praised: great is your power and to your wisdom there is no limit ... for you have made us for yourself, and our heart is restless until it rests in you."

Augustinian Spirituality

At the heart of Augustinian teaching is the Incarnation of Jesus Christ, whom

Augustine calls in one of his sermons the home where we are heading and the way for us to go there. To meet Augustine is to meet another Christ, a fact that may explain the Christo-centricity and intimacy of his *Confessions.*

In a manner typical of the undivided Church of the early ages, Augustine, like all the Fathers, accepted the Bible as the inspired Word of God. This helps to explain why so much of his theologizing is to be found in his sermonizing. Listeners then and readers now will detect in Augustine's work a commitment to both the active and the contemplative life, though clearly for him the fullness of seeing can only be enjoyed in the life to come. Here on earth we continue to see through a glass darkly; only then shall we see face to face!

B

Baptism

This sacrament of initiation marks our entrance into the central mystery of our faith and formation tradition. Baptism is an opening to this ineffable communion with the **Blessed Trinity:** Father, Son, and Holy Spirit.

Baptism forms us in the likeness of Christ, "For in one Spirit we were all baptized into one body" (1 Corinthians 12:13). The white garment worn for this occasion signifies our identification with the risen Lord. The *candle* reminds the participants that those who have "put on Christ" (cf. Galatians 3:27) are to be "the light of the world." The newly baptized are eligible to receive **Confirmation** and first Holy Communion, depending on the practices customary in the Latin or in the Eastern Churches. Regardless of the differences in the rituals surrounding these sacraments, the result is that the baptized are solemnly blessed, drawn into the community of **faith**, and set on the path to graced transformation in Christ, a life described in all its salvific, evangelical, and liturgical splendor in the *Catechism of the Catholic Church* [1248].

Once we are baptized a change happens to us we cannot undo: we are sealed with the indelible spiritual mark (or *character*) of our belonging to Christ. As the *Catechism* teaches, not even sin can erase this mark [1272]. Sin may prevent the grace of Baptism from bearing fruit, but it cannot change our initial configuration to Christ. Therefore, reception of this sacrament cannot be repeated. Once incorporated into the Church, women and men must choose to live and act as committed Christians, giving witness to their consecration to the Lord by the holiness of their lives and the practice of **charity** [1273].

Basil the Great, Saint

(c. 330-79) Along with his friend **Saint Gregory Nazianzus** and his brother **Saint Gregory of Nyssa**, Saint Basil is a Doctor of the universal Church, a Cappadocian Father recognized in the East and in the West as a fierce opponent of **Arianism**. Basil's gifts as a teacher of truth complement his pastoral practices as a devoted bishop and defender of the rights of the poor. Following his ordination to the priesthood, he gave away his inheritance, engaged in social action, and even worked in the soup kitchen he started. To the rich he asked, "How many debtors could be released from prison

Be Filled With Faithfulness

... we should adorn ourselves both from without and from within with virtues and upright behavior, just as the saints did. We should also lovingly and humbly offer up ourselves in God's sight together with all our works. We will thereby meet God through the mediation of all his gifts, be touched with a love that is felt, and be filled with faithfulness toward everyone. In this way we will flow forth and flow back again in true charity and will be firmly established so as to abide in simple peace and likeness to God.

–Blessed John Ruysbroeck

with one of those rings [of yours]?" To the poor he cautioned remembrance of those poorer than they, challenging them to give their last loaf to a beggar at the door and to trust in the providence of God.

Educated in Asia Minor and Athens, this natural-born leader could have pursued a brilliant career as a lawyer, but instead he heard the call to **contemplation**. His sister, Saint Macrina, had already founded a religious community for women at one of their family villas, and Basil wanted to do the same for men. A gifted organizer, Basil wrote his own monastic rule in which he sought to find that happy balance between work and prayer, **solitude** and community. Basil organized the longer and shorter versions of his rule in the form of questions and answers centering on the threefold path of **poverty**, **chastity** (unworldliness), and **obedience**, complemented by practical guidelines for fasting, for hours of **meditation**, study, and labor, and for community prayer. The rules he wrote formed the basis for monastic life in the East and, through **Saint Benedict**, in the West as well.

Beatitudes

These blessings are given by Jesus in his Sermon on the Mount as recorded in the Gospel of Matthew (5:3-12) and in the Gospel of Luke (6:20-23). They constitute the heart of the Master's teaching. Just as the Ten Commandments in the Old Testament summarize the law and the prophets, so the Beatitudes in the New Testament capture the moral obligations and the spiritual longings of the Christian community.

These precious counsels have attracted a wealth of commentary in the writings of the Church Fathers. Both **Saint Augustine** and **Saint Gregory of Nyssa** saw in the Beatitudes a blueprint for Christian perfection, for they contain, in Augustine's words, "all the precepts by which the Christian life has vitality." For **Saint Thomas Aquinas** they offer us a step-by-step itinerary marking our ascent from earth to heaven.

The blessings Jesus gives do not promise us the earthly pleasures associated with self-gratification but the bliss of communion with God through self-giving love. To follow the Beatitudes is to walk the way of the cross. To embrace them as "be-attitudes" or "attitudes of being" is to experience the paradoxical reality of joy in the midst of pain, of **hope** amidst apparent hopelessness. The Lord blesses us as we are here and now, only to confirm how much more we shall become. The Beatitudes intend to build us into a community of persons not burdened by oppressive imperatives but open to the freedom of divine transformation.

Bede the Venerable, Saint

(673-735) A genius with a reputation for modesty, Saint Bede spent the greater part of his life, from youth to old age, with the **Benedictines**. He was a major influence on the Church of the Middle Ages, and is the only Englishman to be named a Doctor of the Church. Of the many books he authored, none was more famous than his *History of the English Church and People*. From his monastery in Northumbria, he chronicled how Christianity came to the British Isles and helped to civilize and unify its diverse people. His accounts of English martyrs and saints, of monarchs and common folk, are so vivid and accurate that some see in them a resemblance to the Acts of the Apostles.

The life and work of Saint Bede demonstrate how Holy Scripture and the teachings of the Church Fathers have the power to draw people to the path of sanctity. His first loves were the study, memorization, and interpretation of the Bible, but his intellectual quest extended as well to such secular fields as mathematics, grammar, and geography. At a time when the Dark Ages were casting a shadow over the Continent, Bede the Venerable was, in the words of Saint Boniface, "the candle of the Church, lit by the Holy Spirit."

His last great act was to translate the Gospel of John into the vernacular. These parting words of his offer a fitting epitaph to his life of fidelity: "I pray you, noble Jesus, that as you have graciously granted me joyfully to imbibe the words of your knowledge, so you will also of your bounty grant me to come at length to yourself, the fount of all wisdom, and to dwell in your presence forever."

Benedict of Nursia, Saint

(480-543) Lauded in the annals of Church history as the Father of Western monasticism, Benedict lived at a time when Western civilization itself was at the threshold of death. The Roman Empire was crumbling under a barrage of barbarian invasions; wars devastated his native Italy; famine and disease ravaged the land. None of these forces, however, could dim the radiance of this future saint.

Born and educated near Rome, Benedict and his twin sister, Saint Scholastica, were members of a noble family, but neither clung to privilege. In fact, so degraded did the young Benedict feel by the lax moral atmosphere around him that he sought the bracing air of **solitude**. He fled from the city, as had his desert counterparts like **Saint Antony of Egypt** and **John Cassian**, to the solitude of his hermitage at Subiaco. Benedict would have been content to spend the rest of his days there, but God had other plans for him.

A nearby community of monks asked the holy man to be their abbot. **Saint Gregory the Great** reveals in his *Dialogue* that a jealous priest attempted to poison him, but literally died trying. Disheartened by this episode, Benedict took it as a sign from God that he should be a hermit. What he did not count on was the fact that many disciples decided to follow him and that soon their numbers would grow so fast that he would have to found his own monastery. It was on the heights of Monte Cassino, around 525, that the Benedictine way of life began in earnest.

Many miracles were attributed to the founder, but perhaps the greatest and most long-lasting one was the composition of his *Rule*. Age upon age religious have turned to *The Rule of Saint Benedict* for vocational discernment, inspiration, and practical application in the realm of work and prayer. Behind every act of **charity**, one who follows the *Rule* will find the Christlike attitudes of **obedience**, inner **silence**, stability, and **humility**. The *opus dei*, the work of God, is first of all the practice of liturgical prayer from which flows filial love, **compunction** of heart, awareness of God's presence, moderation, and respect for each person's life call.

Though Benedictine life has had to suffer through the ups and downs of decline and reform, it remains an inspiration to laity, clergy, and religious, who hear in the very Prologue to the *Rule* the call to form, reform, and transform their lives:

> Listen carefully, my son, to the master's instructions, and attend to them with the ear of your heart. This is advice from a father who loves you; welcome it, and faithfully put it into practice. The labor of obedience will

bring you back to him from whom you had drifted through the sloth of disobedience. This message of mine is for you, then, if you are ready to give up your own will, once and for all, and armed with the strong and noble weapons of obedience to do battle for the true King, Christ the Lord.

Benedictine Spirituality

In spite of the changing ways and altered conditions of modern monastic life, the Benedictine ideal has remained unchanged: to integrate the love of God with the works of **charity** owed to one's neighbor. A true Christian community in the Benedictine sense is always a "school of charity." The *Rule* embodies the wisdom of the **Desert Fathers**, notably **Saint Antony of Egypt** and **John Cassian**. A typical trait of Benedictine spirituality is its stress on meditation and **contemplation** as the sources of Christian action.

Clergy, religious, and laity who follow the Benedictine way know that the love of learning must be subordinated to the desire for God and that the acquisition of spiritual knowledge and discipline begins with **obedience** to Christ. One adopts a posture of discipleship in relation to one's spiritual father or mother, the abbot or abbess invested with legitimate authority. **Conversion** and submission, perseverance in the common life, and confidence in God—all strengthen moral conduct and ready one for conformity to Christ. This relationship with the living God prevails whether one adheres to the *Rule* as an individual or in community. Benedict assimilated essential spiritual rhythms such as prayer and work, discretion and self-discipline, obedience and originality, **humility** and creativity, **compunction** and the confidence of filial love. What matters is not outer consent to the *Rule* but inner change of heart.

To the Church as a whole, Benedictine spirituality has left the legacy of the fourfold path of *lectio divina* (sacred reading); *meditatio* (meditation on the Word of God); *oratio* (vocal and mental prayer); and *contemplatio* (acquired and infused contemplation) that flows over into *actio* (charitable service in Christ's name). So deeply is this practice rooted in the Church's tradition that several centuries after Benedict, **Saint John of the Cross** was able to condense its richness into one sentence: "Seek in reading and you will find in meditation; knock in prayer and it shall be opened to you in contemplation."

Bernadette of Lourdes, Saint
(1844-79) Bernadette's visions of the **Blessed Virgin Mary** have made her village one of the most famous pilgrimage sites in the world.

In 1858, at the age of fourteen, this uneducated French girl was the recipient of eighteen apparitions of Mary in a rocky grotto near her home. "I am the Immaculate Conception," the Virgin Mary proclaimed to Bernadette. The doctrine of the Immaculate Conception had been formally defined by Pope Pius IX in 1854. Bernadette still suffered much scrutiny and endless questioning about what she saw. However, the young visionary maintained her dignity. The main message Mary conveyed to her was: "Pray and do penance for the conversion of the world." There, too, Bernadette received the command to build a church.

Many churches have now been built around the grotto to accommodate the three million or so pilgrims who visit Lourdes every year. At this place of awe and wonder, a miraculous spring appeared whose healing waters still flow. A medical bureau, established in 1882, tests to this day the authenticity of the cures said to be received. (No cure is ever authenticated as miraculous if science can show any natural explanation of it.)

Simple a soul as she was, Bernadette could not have foreseen the full measure of her visions nor the immense graces that would flow from them. She herself joined the Sisters of Charity of Nevers, where she found a happy home until her death.

Bernard of Clairvaux, Saint
(1090-1153) Over the ages Bernard has garnered many superlative titles, including author of the Cistercian reform, the last of the Fathers, counselor of popes and kings, ecclesiastical statesman and diplomat, mediator between warring factions, and Doctor of the Church. For good reason, this prolific author and abbot was perhaps the most influential person in Europe during the first half of the twelfth century.

Bernard was born and educated in Dijon, France. Like his mentor, **Saint Benedict**, he could have pursued a destiny fitting his noble upbringing. Instead in 1113 he felt drawn to enter the newly reformed monastery of Cîteaux. His gifts of persuasion were obvious even then, for he had no trouble convincing thirty of his relatives and friends to enter with him. Under the guidance of the Holy Spirit, they transformed a community on the verge of extinction into a vibrant movement in the Church that would eventually spawn over three hundred houses across the whole of Europe.

One of the daughter houses of

Cîteaux was in the town of Clairvaux. There Bernard became abbot. Though he would have been content to live a hidden life of work and prayer, his reputation for wisdom and holiness soon spread beyond the boundaries of his monastery, drawing him into the thick of ecclesial and political affairs, including the preaching of the Second Crusade. Bernard might well be called, in the same breath with **Saint Augustine** and **Saint John of the Cross**, a Doctor of Love. It should come as no surprise that at the end of the *Divine Comedy* Dante chose as his spiritual guide to "the Love that moves the sun and other stars" none other than Saint Bernard, who once said, "My purpose is not so much to explain words [as] to move hearts."

Blessed Trinity

These words, so full of awe and mystery, express the central tenet of our faith. Belief in the Most Blessed Trinity differentiates Christianity from monotheistic **faith** traditions like Judaism and Islam. We are baptized and we make the sign of the cross "in the name of the Father and of the Son and of the Holy Spirit."

One God in Three Persons—this revelation is, according to the *Catechism*, "the source of all the other mysteries of faith, the light that enlightens them" [234]. Such knowledge is inaccessible to human reason. Not even Israel's faith could accommodate a mystery as profound as the Incarnation. When we recite the Nicene Creed, we confess the truth that Jesus is the only-begotten Son of God, that he is "eternally begotten of the Father, light from light, true God from true God, begotten, not made, one in Being with the Father." This truth has been revealed to us by the Third Person of the Blessed Trinity, the Holy Spirit, whom Jesus calls our Advocate. As we pray in the Creed, "We believe in the Holy Spirit, the Lord and giver of life, who proceeds from the Father and the Son." All Three Persons of the Trinity share the same substance and the same nature. Thus, together with the Father and the Son, the Holy Spirit "is worshipped and glorified."

The early Church Fathers, at the Council of Nicea in 325, and again at the Fourth Lateran Council in 1215, defended this bulwark of our faith against any and all errors that sought to deform it. We hear this sacred doctrine summarized many times over in the Church, and nowhere more frequently than in the greeting we hear in the Eucharistic liturgy when the priest says: "The grace of the Lord Jesus Christ and the love of God and the fellowship of the Holy Spirit be with you all."

Bonaventure, Saint

(c. 1221-74) A cardinal and a Doctor of the Church, Bonaventure was both a loyal follower of **Saint Francis of Assisi** and his principal biographer. He saw in his mentor a living example of what it meant to adhere wholly to God. In his book on the life and times of the Poor Man of God, Bonaventure tells how he experienced the power of the saint's intercession through a miraculous cure. Inspired to join the Franciscans in his youth, Bonaventure was sent to study in Paris, where he forged a lifelong friendship with **Saint Thomas Aquinas**, a Dominican friar who, like him, upheld the founder's vision of preaching the faith to the masses rather than living and working only in a monastery.

A man whose immense intellect matched his equally immense **humility**, Bonaventure wrote what many consider to be the most complete synthesis of Christian **mysticism** ever composed, his masterpiece on *The Soul's Journey into God*. In this book he traces six degrees of ascent to mystical union, using the metaphor of the six-winged seraph. In the first two stages the soul seeks God through the senses, as he may be found in his creation. In the next two phases one turns within to contemplate God through his image imprinted on one's own powers of memory, intellect, and will, an image that has to be reformed and purified in the fourth stage by the virtues of **faith**, **hope**, and **charity.** In the last two stages of the journey, the soul rises above itself to behold the Divine Unity that points in reality to the **Blessed Trinity**. Having reached the perfection of this illumination, the soul is ready to pass from this life to the next in the wonder of the Beatific Vision. No symbol for this itinerary is more convincing to Bonaventure than Saint Francis' own experience of receiving the stigmata on Mount Alverno as a prelude to his final *transitus* to eternity.

In 1257 Bonaventure was elected minister general of the Franciscan Order. For the next sixteen years, in addition to holding this defining position of servant leadership, he worked hard to heal the divisions in his own Franciscan house, realizing in his life and his writings how difficult it is to integrate the love of learning with the desire for God.

Bosco, Saint John

(1815-88) Born near the city of Turin in the Piedmont region of Italy, John was only two years old when his father died. This loss meant that the boy's life of labor on the family farm had just begun. As John grew older, something else happened to him. He received the extraordinary grace of dream visions, the accuracy of which history would prove. By the age of ten, the theme of his life, "Give me souls!" began to emerge. He knew he was called to the priesthood, but since there was no money to send him to school, John had to support himself by working in a blacksmith shop, then as a tailor, a waiter, a shoemaker, and even a pin-boy in a bowling alley. Jobs like this gave him the invaluable experience he needed for his later work among disadvantaged boys. In one of John's dreams, a fight broke out and a man said to him, "You will never help these boys by beating them. Be kind to them, teach them that sin is evil and that purity is a precious gift."

John finally finished his studies and went to the seminary, where he is credited with a reputation for scholarly excellence and piety. He was ordained to the priesthood on June 5, 1841. From that moment, it was as if God had released through him a powerful spiritual energy. Caring for poor and abandoned youth became his life-consuming mission. He began this ministry in the slums of Turin, where despicable poverty, child labor, and starvation wages abounded. There Don Bosco, as he came to be called, found what Christ really wanted of him: "These boys were not bad at one time. Take care of them before they fall into crime—that is your task!" And so it was that he educated abandoned youngsters, tended to their basic needs, and brought a sense of **peace** to their restless souls.

By 1859, with the help of his own students, he formed the Salesian Society, named after **Saint Francis de Sales**, a man whose virtues of gentleness, kindness, and patience appealed to Don Bosco. After the death of their beloved founder, this society came to be known as the Salesians. With the help of Sister Mary Mazzarello, Don Bosco also founded the Daughters of Mary, Help of Christians, to do similar work among girls. Also, before his death, he was guided by other dream-visions to open works outside of Italy, which today span the world.

At Don Bosco's canonization on April 1, 1934, Pope Pius XI said: "Don Bosco is one of those great meteors that sweep from time to time across the vault of heaven and leave a long trail, shedding seeds of life, of goodness, and of peace."

Cabrini, Saint Frances Xavier
(1850-1917) This remarkable, modern-day missionary was born in the province of Lombardy, Italy, but a "stay at home" she was not! Her travels would rival those of Saint Paul. Just as he traveled from one Mediterranean port to another, making converts along the way, so this petite school teacher with a passionate heart would cross and recross the sea, overcoming her fear of water and making a total of twenty-five voyages. These travels yielded over sixty new foundations and the growth of her order, the Missionary Sisters of the Sacred Heart, whose houses can be found in Italy, France, Spain, and England, in the United States, and in Central and South America.

Mother Cabrini, as this foundress was fondly called, was a living witness to God's strength surpassing every human weakness, of his fidelity working best in human frailty. There was in her life a constant synthesis of **contemplation** and action. Though her character was introverted and reserved, she was known for her exceptional friendliness and organizational skill. Already as a child she felt as if she belonged to God in a manner similar to the experiences of **Saint Catherine of Siena** and **Saint Thérèse of Lisieux**. She was captivated by a **devotion** to the Sacred Heart, desiring in her person and mission to love the suffering and to suffer for love.

Cabrini's special affection extended to the lost and lonely, to those abandoned in body and in soul. Wherever human beings merely subsist at the margins of society, there she wanted her sisters to be found. Her work with hospitals, schools, and orphanages as well as her motherly commitment to clothe and feed the homeless and poor was without precedent, so much so that her great personal friend, Pope Leo XIII, said to her on one occasion, "Let us work, Cabrini, and we will win heaven." It was in New York City, caring for hundreds of Italian immigrants, that Mother Cabrini understood the real meaning of pastoral ministry: to heal every form of human misery and to bring the reign of God into every human heart.

Call to Holiness
The Dogmatic Constitution of the Church (*Lumen Gentium*, 1964) is the Vatican Council II document in which we read:

> … all Christians in any state or walk of life are called to the fullness of

> Christian life and to the perfection of love, and by this holiness a more human manner of life is fostered also in earthly society.

This text announces what has since become known as the "universal call to holiness," a call issued in a special way to the laity by the Council Fathers, who said that the "People of God" share in their own way in "the priestly, prophetic and kingly office of Christ, and to the best of their ability carry on the mission of the whole Christian people in the Church and in the world."

It is in the temporal affairs of the world—in the work of business and commerce, of family and social life—that we must hear the call of God to live holy and productive lives in the spirit of the Gospel, fulfilling the duties and responsibilities associated with our vocation, so that the saving light of Jesus Christ may be brought to the whole of human society through the members of Christ's body, the Church. Whatever our obligations, whatever our degree of success or failure, wealth or poverty, fame or hiddenness, our call comes from God and beckons us to return to God. As *Lumen Gentium* says in summary, quoting **Saint John Chrysostom,** "In a word: 'what the soul is in the body, let Christians be in the world.'"

Capital Sins

Sin distorts the likeness that ought to exist between God and us. As we read in the Book of Genesis (1: 26-27), God made us, male and female, in his image, after his likeness. According to **Saint John of the Cross,** while we remain in substantial union with God by virtue of our creation, we drift away from him into the land of unlikeness by virtue of our sinfulness. This proclivity to sin engenders a perverse repetition of vices that clouds our conscience and our ability to choose between good and evil.

Just as the living of a virtuous life strengthens our innate moral sense, so the choice of vice weakens it. To describe this basic disorientation and the pattern of vice it connotes, spiritual writers like **Saint Augustine**, **Saint Gregory the Great**, and **John Cassian** identify the capital sins—so called because they loosen a veritable avalanche of other more or less grave sins. The *Catechism of the Catholic Church* lists these main ways of missing the mark: "pride, avarice, envy, wrath, lust, gluttony, and sloth or acedia" [1866].

To give just one example of sin's malicious proliferation, lust may breed fornication, impurity, licentiousness, lack of modesty, and carousing. Because such acts are ultimately self-gratifying and self-centered, it is understandable that the most fundamental of the capital sins is pride or arrogant self-esteem. It destroys awe for God and prompts us to reject our dependence on his grace for the very possibility of salvation.

Carmelite Spirituality

This special avenue to union with God began in earnest with the reform initiated by **Saint Teresa of Avila** in the sixteenth century. However, the roots of this movement can be traced to Mount Carmel in Palestine at the time of Elijah the prophet. His hunger for God alone can still be felt in the souls of Carmelite women and men who have been called to go apart in **solitude**, to detach themselves from traditional roles in society, and to serve the Lord in prayer and communal participation. In the Middle Ages, Teresian reform was prompted by the mitigation of the rule originally governing the Carmelite order from the time it was composed in 1209, by Saint Albert, Patriarch of Jerusalem.

Under the leadership of Saint Teresa and **Saint John of the Cross** emerged the Discalced (or "shoeless," symbolic of their poverty) Carmelites. While reform meant change—for example, a more simplified, cloistered lifestyle—what remained unchanged was the founding spirit of the order: to restore the soul's center in God through renunciation of self.

Saints like **Thérèse of Lisieux** and more recently **Saint Teresa Benedicta of the Cross** (Edith Stein) dispel the myth that contemplatives have only a minor role to play in the Church's mission of evangelization. Nothing could be further from the truth. The spirituality of Carmel proves that one's commitment to **contemplation** is an essential bridge to evangelization. The Carmelite way, in its apostolic and contemplative, active and cloistered traditions, upholds the need to reach out to God and others in the darkness of **faith**. Neither **consolation** nor **desolation**, neither sensory perception nor ecstatic experiences, are the goals of the spiritual life. God must lift the human spirit in its nakedness into the way of union, symbolized by mystical marriage. (See **Mysticism.**)

Carthusian Spirituality

This **charism** finds its roots in the love for **silence** and **solitude,** which inspired the first desert dwellers in Egypt and Syria in the early Christian era. Founded by Saint Bruno in Italy in 1084, this order of contemplative monks began at the same time as Saint Robert of Molesmes founded the **Cistercians**. Though Robert's reformed monastery at Cîteaux returned to strict observance of *The Rule of Saint Benedict*, Bruno preferred to follow an even stricter style of life. Under the jurisdiction of the bishop of Grenoble, he and six of his companions settled in the mountainous terrain of Chartreuse in France. There they built the first of their simple huts near the chapel, seeking isolation as Jesus did when he went alone to a quiet place to pray (cf. Matthew 14:23).

Lay brothers joined the hermits to attend to their needs, since their lives were by choice simple, silent, solitary, and austere, forbidding visitors and declining proprietary obligations. A community normally numbers only twelve members, in imitation of the first apostles. The monks emulate the eremitical way of monasticism in the desert, and live in individual cells or cottages. They follow in silence and solitude a regular schedule of prayer, **spiritual reading**, manual labor, gardening, eating, and sleeping. The monks do assemble for worship on Sundays and feast days. They pray the Divine Office together and share two meals daily. On weekdays they also sing Holy Mass, Vespers, Matins, and Lauds in church.

As viable an order today as when it was founded, Carthusians are full of apostolic **zeal**, concern for neighborly love, and care for the brethren. These ideals are an integral part of their spiritual exercises, daily prayers, and labors. The strength of the order and its viability in the Church comes not so much from scholarship as from **contemplative prayer** and the witness of holy lives, of both monks and nuns, touching something of eternity on earth.

Cassian, John

(c. 360-435) Cassian was a disciple of **Evagrius Ponticus** in the East and a contemporary of **Saint Augustine** in the West. He spent his early days in religion under the tutelage of the **Desert Fathers.** A pupil of **Saint John Chrysostom**, Cassian entered a monastery in Bethlehem before leaving to study monasticism in Egypt along with his friend and fellow monk, Germanus. In later years, following his ordination, Cassian became a major force in the formation of Western monastic spirituality. **Saint Benedict** acknowledges the lasting influence of his great works, *The Institutes*, for beginners in the monastic life, and *The Conferences*, for more advanced souls seeking to be "ideal" monks.

With his background and experience in Eastern monasticism and his first-hand acquaintance with eremetical and cenobitical life, Cassian was able to found his own monastery near Marseilles for men and one nearby for women. Out of a diversity of Egyptian influences, traceable to other teachers of his, notably **Saint Maximus the Confessor** and **Origen**, he began to create a coherent scheme of spirituality.

The way to God, for Cassian, was a

perpetual spiritual combat, a struggle to divest the soul of vices, of all transient, egocentric, and material interests, by means of the virtues initiated by God's grace and nurtured by **solitude, compunction**, and uninterrupted communion with God. He insisted, as did Saint Benedict, that the essence of perfection is **charity** and that the perfection of charity is reached by way of **asceticism**—not as a goal in itself but as a means toward greater love and unceasing **contemplative prayer**.

A lover of God's Word all his life, a teacher known for his eloquence, Cassian was particularly fond of psalmody, not merely sung or said but assimilated into the very marrow of one's being until it gave birth to mystical prayer that could transform the heart and light up for the believer the Bible's whole meaning. One must develop, in his words, a "passion for the unseen" and tend always toward union with God. Cassian's ascetic ideals remain grounded in a genial, realistic sense of everydayness, of the need for **humility**, discretion, common sense, and moderation—all of which may explain why, when he died, he had already attained the reputation of being a saint.

Catherine of Genoa, Saint

(1447-1510) A layperson, a married woman, and a paragon of **charity**, Catherine of Genoa united in her life and work **contemplation** and action. At once a mystic and a humanitarian, a contemplative and a servant, Saint Catherine immersed herself in caring for the physically ill and destitute.

Born into a noble family of wealth and prestige—two of her ancestors were popes—Catherine was an elegant, attractive woman, who strove from an early age to practice simplicity. She also had to grapple with feelings of overwhelming grief that would overtake her when she thought of God's sufferings for sinners. She recognized in her own soul an "instinct for beatitude," a restlessness that could only come to rest in God in this life and the next.

Though Catherine wanted to enter religious life, she had to submit to her parents' will that she marry at the age of sixteen a Genoese nobleman whose character was the opposite of her own. For the next ten years of her life she suffered over his dissolute ways. Though her life was lonely, she tried to see in it Divine Providence's way of granting her a taste of the eremitical life she had always wanted to live. In 1473 her husband abandoned her altogether, though by that time Catherine had become quite ill. In March of that year, when death seemed to be knocking at her door, she was the recipient of a singular act of God's grace: sudden illuminations that would change her forever. God pierced her heart and showed her the depth of misery and sin from which his Son had saved her.

Lent and Advent became special times in Catherine's life. She fasted for forty days. Her only food was the **Eucharist** and a little salty water. Miraculously, her strength did not waver. She devoted herself to charitable works and penitential acts. Gradually, over the next four years, these mortifications ceased, except for her fasting which she said was a work of God independent of her own will. Around 1480 she was appointed matron of the hospital of Genoa. Soon thereafter her husband returned to her, a repentant man, who also wanted to devote himself to care of the sick. Catherine's own untiring energy served her and the ill especially well during the Plague that ravaged Genoa in 1493. In 1496, failing health forced her to retire as matron, but she gathered around her a core of devoted laity and clergy, who formed an Oratory of Divine Love to foster spiritual reform and to provide for the poor. In the presence of her friends and followers, she would discourse on the love of God and the affections for him burning in her heart. On November 11, 1509, having tasted purgatory on earth and expelled every trace of self-love, Catherine died in the **peace** and joy awaiting every pure soul.

Catherine of Siena, Saint

(1347-80) The twenty-fourth of twenty-five children of a prosperous Sienese family, Catherine of Siena was destined to become the patron saint of Italy and one of three women (along with **Teresa of Avila** and **Thérèse of Lisieux**) named a Doctor of the Church. At the age of six Catherine had a vision of Christ the King that changed the direction of her life forever. Despite her parents' wishes, she refused to marry, cutting off her golden hair as a sign that she would remain a virgin, to be wed only to her heavenly spouse.

In her teenage years, she lived as a contemplative in her own home and was the recipient of many graces associated with mystical espousal and marriage, a favor granted to her in 1367. Unschooled and illiterate, Catherine somehow learned to read through the intervention of the Holy Spirit. Though she remained a laywoman, serving Christ in the world, she sought communal affiliation with the Sisters of Penitence under the sponsorship of the Dominican Order. Like their founder, **Saint Thomas Aquinas**, Catherine wanted above all to know and teach the truth, to practice **charity**, and to adore the presence of Christ in the **Eucharist**.

Slowly, as she passed into her adult years, Catherine heard and obeyed the Lord's command to leave her solitude and reach out to the needy of Siena, to its prisoners, to the sick and the poor.

By 1370 her world had expanded to include people from all walks of life, popes and counselors as well as common folk. She was enlisted as a peacemaker when anarchy reigned in Siena, as a healer and spiritual director, and even as a brilliant negotiator when she was asked to approach Pope Gregory XI to return from Avignon to Rome. His successor, Urban VI, also recognized in Catherine a powerful advocate. He appointed her papal emissary to the city-states in revolt. At the beginning of the Great Schism in 1378, Pope Urban called her to Rome, but her efforts to prevent this tear in the fabric of the Church were in vain.

So weary was she of these attempts to restore unity that she died in Rome in her thirty-third year, leaving a legacy of transcribed letters (over four hundred written to leaders of both Church and State); a series of poems celebrating her love for the **Blessed Trinity** and her union with the Risen Lord; and, most importantly, her masterpiece on the spiritual life, *The Dialogue*. Its central theme is God's truth, of which the soul seeks a deeper understanding not through intellectual mastery but through that humility of mind that is born of pure faith.

Celibacy

Toward the end of the sixth century, celibacy became a regular discipline in the Western Church for women and men living the religious life in community or alone in the world. In that same era, Pope Gregory the Great mandated celibacy to be lived as a sign of new life in service of the Church for all clerics in major orders.

It is a Church discipline established by ecclesiastical law in the Latin Rite that clergy accept with a free and joyous heart the obligation to remain single, and to live a life of **chastity** in imitation of Christ. In the Eastern Church married men can be ordained as deacons and priests while bishops are chosen solely from among celibates. In both the West and the East, a man who has already received the sacrament of Holy Orders can no longer marry.

Celibacy, however, is more than a state of *not* being married; it is a full and deeply loving way of life, embraced by clergy, religious, and laity living the single life in the world as a way, in the words of the *Catechism*, to consecrate oneself "with an undivided heart to the Lord and to the 'affairs of the Lord'" [1579]. It is a radiant proclamation that the reign of God is at hand and that "the world in its present form is passing away"(1 Corinthians 7:31).

Centering Prayer

One important contemporary revival of a method of prayer, as old as Christianity itself, is that of "centering prayer." It was first taught in the West by **John Cassian**, who wrote about a method of coming to rest in God in his *Conferences* that consists of the faithful reiteration of the Psalmist's plea: "O God, come to my assistance; O Lord, make haste to help me." This way of prayer also traces its roots to a medieval text by the anonymous author of ***The Cloud of Unknowing***, where it is said that few words and firm love lead us most swiftly to God. Important in this tradition is its insistence that **contemplative prayer** is meant for all and not only for a chosen few.

The guidelines to centering prayer, offered by the National Office of Contemplative Outreach, a group begun by Abbot Thomas Keating, are basic: (1) Choose a sacred word as the symbol of your intention to consent to God's presence and action within. (2) Sit comfortably and with eyes closed, settle briefly, and silently introduce the sacred word as the symbol of your consent to God's presence and action within. (3) When you become aware of thoughts, return ever so gently to the sacred word. (4) At the end of the prayer period, remain in silence with eyes closed for a couple of minutes, and perhaps end the centering prayer session, usually after a duration of twenty minutes, by the slow recitation of the **Lord's Prayer**.

In regard to judging the authenticity of this or any form of contemplative prayer, its practitioners would agree with **Thomas Merton** that "the life of contemplation is ... not simply a life of human technique and discipline; it is the life of the Holy Spirit in our inmost souls."

Charism

The Greek word *charismata* designates special graces and benefits of the Holy Spirit granted to an individual for the sanctification of others. The *Catechism* defines charisms as favors or gratuitous gifts, like miracles of healing or speaking in tongues, "oriented toward sanctifying grace and ... intended for the common good of the Church" [2003].

One who receives such graces accepts them gladly as from the hand of God, even with the crosses that at times accompany them, not the least of which may be some form of persecution or misunderstanding. Charisms are reservoirs of apostolic vitality and reminders of the **call to holiness** for all members of Christ's Mystical Body. The authority of the Church provides a safeguard against abuses of these gifts by testing them to ensure that they are in full conformity to the Holy Spirit's promptings.

Undoubtedly, the true measure of all charisms, as Saint Paul tells us in First Corinthians 13, is **charity**.

Charismatic Spirituality

This special charism emerges from the Catholic Pentecostal Movement. Its keynote is the baptism of the Holy Spirit, a deeply moving experience through which one feels renewed by God's Spirit and overflowing with graces that for some take the form of healing (physical or otherwise) or the ability to speak in tongues. Groups of people touched by the Holy Spirit meet frequently to pray, praise the Lord, sing and share the Good News, and offer personal testimony to the **faith** that fills them. Like all special schools of spirituality, this way suits some people, but it is not *the* way for all Christians to follow.

The Catholic Charismatic Renewal gained momentum in the 1960s, starting with the efforts of the Chi-Rho Society of Duquesne University in Pittsburgh, Pennsylvania. In the 1970s, the University of Notre Dame was the site of international prayer meetings and further promulgation of the movement. It came under the scrutiny of the Catholic hierarchy to ensure that members remained faithful to the common ways of **spiritual formation** in the Church and to her authority in theological matters, and that they avoided any espousal of biblical fundamentalism or exclusivity. It was determined that a sense of renewed fervor for a life of prayer, apostolic **zeal**, and community commitment, including ecumenical outreach and social action, are commendable attributes of charismatic spirituality.

Unofficial papal approval of the movement can be traced to the year 1975, when ten thousand charismatics came to Rome and were received by Pope Paul VI, under the watchful and devoted eye of Cardinal Suenens of Belgium, a strong proponent of the movement. Later Pope John Paul II concurred with his predecessor's approval, thus suggesting that this new school of spirituality may have a lasting place in the life of the Church. If so, it will provide for its adherents a special bridge that links the foundations of the faith to a distinct way and style of personalizing them. Charismatics focus on the indwelling of the Holy Spirit through which the presence of Christ, risen and glorified, is revealed.

In combined meetings held in 1971 and 1972 between Vatican officials and representatives of various Pentecostal movements, a joint statement said that this experience "is not a goal to be reached, nor a place to stand, but a door through which to go into a greater fullness of life in the Spirit. It is an event that becomes a way of life in which often-charismatic manifestations have a place. Characteristic of this way of life is a love of the word of God, and a concern to live by the power of the Spirit."

Charity

This divinely infused theological virtue disposes us to prefer God as the highest, most sovereign good in our life, and to place our love for him and our desire to obey his will above all else. *Caritas*, the Latin word for charity, suggests a movement of the heart that calls us to seek union and communion with the **Blessed Trinity**. This foremost love is the light that guides our faithful adherence to the first part of the Great Commandment. It empowers us to pour forth love for our neighbor for God's sake.

By contrast, sin is an offense against and a failure in genuine love for God and neighbor. So serious is this matter that the *Catechism* defines mortal sin as that which "destroys charity in the heart of man by a grave violation of God's law," and venial sin as that which "allows charity to subsist, even though it offends and wounds it" [1855].

What a stark contrast to sin is the selfless, self-giving love of charity! It is the royal road to heaven and the way on earth to become more like Jesus. He loved us so much that he offered his life in atonement for our transgressions. The apostle Paul is unambiguous when it comes to the centrality of this virtue. Everything partial, from prophecy to knowledge, passes away, he says. Only **faith**, **hope**, and love remain, but of these three, the greatest virtue is love (1 Corinthians 13:13). However varied the gifts and demands of the apostolate may be, all vocations can be traced to the same source. It is, as the *Catechism* assures us, "charity, drawn from the **Eucharist**." This is "the soul of the whole apostolate" [864].

Chastity

This moral virtue sustains our efforts to control the impulses and compulsions of human sexuality in accordance with right reason and the law of God. It excludes in both married and single persons any sinful indulgences that arise from sexuality severed from the guiding light of a fully formed and informed conscience. Of course, the way chastity expresses itself in these two states of life differs accordingly, but every human being, aided by grace, ought to commit him or herself to love self and others in a nonabusive, chaste, and respectful way. That is why Jesus teaches his followers to be not only chaste in body but in mind as well: "You have heard that it was said, 'You shall not commit adultery.' But I say to you, everyone who looks at a woman with lust has already committed adultery with her in his heart" (Matthew 5:27-28).

A person who makes a vow of chastity or a solemn or simple promise not to enter into the state of matrimony chooses to remain celibate for the sake of the kingdom. Such is the commitment asked of the ordained and of women and men who live a consecrated life in community or in the world. In addition to the perfection of charity to which all the faithful are called by virtue of their Baptism, other Christians (religious living in community, hermits, consecrated virgins, and dedicated single persons) practice chaste, respectful love in a life dedicated totally to God. According to the *Catechism*, "'Their witness of a Christian life' aims 'to order temporal things according to God and inform the world with the power of the gospel'" [929].[1]

Far from being merely a negative state of not being married, celibacy is a joyful lifestyle that enables a person to be more wholly present to, more inclusively loving of, the brothers and sisters who cross one's path. As the *Catechism* reminds us, "Whether their witness is public, as in the religious state, or less public, or even secret, Christ's coming remains for all those consecrated both the origin and rising sun of their life" [933].

Cistercian Spirituality

This special school of spirituality emanated from the life of the monks of the Order of Cîteaux founded in 1098 by Saint Robert of Molesmes, whose intention was to follow a more strict observance of the **Benedictine** rule. In due course this reform movement branched into two streams. Following the strictest way of life were the Trappists, who practice perpetual silence, except when it is necessary to speak; who abstain from meat, fish, and poultry, except for health reasons; and whose primary work is farming and food production. Following the common observance with some modification of the original rule of **Saint Benedict** are, for example, orders of Cistercian nuns like the Bernardines, who also live cloistered, contemplative lives.

Practicing a kind of communal or corporate **solitude**, followers of the tradition of Cîteaux move away from populous areas while staying committed to one another in a manner in keeping with a community's unique Cistercian spirit. By choosing to settle in places removed from so-called civilized life, the monks and nuns have ample opportunity for the manual labor emphasized in *The Rule of Saint Benedict*. Working the land and following a rigorous regimen of prayer and **spiritual reading**, guided by the **Liturgy of the Hours**, contribute to such Cistercian traits as simplicity, **silence**, devotionality, fasting, and **poverty**—all destined to draw the soul into closer union with Father, Son, and Holy Spirit through obedience to the Rule and customs of the order.

Cistercians share a great love both for our Lord and his mother, the **Blessed Virgin Mary**. They seek through her intercession the grace of ongoing conversion, since the worldliness of the world of commerce and trade, noise, and notoriety is never far away. For all the struggle authentic solitude entails, the love and joy it evokes are great. **William of Saint Thierry** felt this way when he met **Saint Bernard of Clairvaux** and was drawn by his example to the Cistercian reform flourishing in France in the twelfth century. He wrote in one of his meditations on the Song of Songs a prayer with which his fellow monks could readily identify: "O you who have willed to be called charity, give me charity, that I may love you more than I love myself, not caring at all what I do with myself, so long as I am doing what is pleasing in your sight."

Ciszek, Father Walter

(1904-84) A Jesuit priest, confessor, and spiritual director whose faith journey produced two contemporary classics, *With God in Russia* and *He Leadeth Me*, Father Walter grew up in Shenandoah, a quiet mining town in eastern Pennsylvania. Home to many immigrants, it now counts Father Walter as its most precious supernatural resource. He left home against his father's wishes to join the Society of Jesus in 1928, but religious fervor and deep faith were not foreign to his family; two of his sisters became Bernardine sisters. His initial formation in family life left him with the strong impression that great good can come from suffering and tragedy as long as one lives in **abandonment to Divine Providence** and never ceases trusting in God's will.

During his time of preparation for the priesthood, Father Walter volunteered to study Russian in the hope of being missioned to the Soviet Union. He had even been ordained in the Russian Byzantine Rite in June of 1937. Instead he found himself on assignment in eastern Poland in 1938, where within a year he watched as Red Army troops invaded the country. Ciszek, with the **faith** that has become his badge of honor, saw the hand of God in this event. He joined the Polish refugees disguised as a worker.

Transported to the labor camps of Russia, he intended to carry on his ministry in secret, but two years later he was arrested by the Soviet secret police, sentenced to fifteen years of hard labor, and incarcerated in solitary confinement for five years in the notorious Lubianka Prison in Moscow, where his captors determined to wrest from him his confession as a spy. His days in prison were like one long unbroken chain of harassment by the secret police, who eventually broke his will and forced him to sign a confession full of lies. But this breakdown of the last remnant of his personal pride was the breakthrough to complete **humility** he needed to excel in heroic virtue for Christ's sake.

After serving in full his sentence of fifteen years of hard labor, he was suddenly released in 1963 as part of a prisoner exchange. Ciszek returned to his community in New York City, where he lived as a member of the John XXIII Center for Eastern Christian Studies at Fordham University for the remaining twenty years of his life. There he served as a spiritual guide and a saintly witness to the merits gained through a trial by faith. He freely shared with all who sought his counsel a word of **hope** and the secret of his peace and joy: "I had to have constant recourse to prayer, to the eyes of faith, to a humility that could make me aware of how little my own efforts meant and how dependent I was upon God's grace even for prayer and faith itself." He died at the age of eighty on the Feast of the Immaculate Conception, a good and faithful servant, ready to enjoy the banquet his Master had prepared for him.

Clare of Assisi, Saint

(c. 1193-1254) The beloved daughter of a noble Italian family, Clare refused two offers of marriage, but did not finally make up her mind to leave the world until she came under the influence of the Poor Man of God, **Saint Francis of Assisi**. When Clare was eighteen, she left home secretly under Francis' direction. She had heard him preach a sermon and from then on never wavered in her determination to emulate him and to live a life of strict **poverty** herself.

On Passion Sunday, 1212, leaving her home and all its worldly advantages, she went to the place where Francis lived with his community. Here she found her home in heaven while yet on earth. Before the altar in the little church, she received the habit from the hand of Francis. He placed her in the care of a local convent of Benedictine nuns. Her family tried to induce her to return home, but in vain. She was joined by her younger sister, Agnes, and later by her widowed mother and another sister. Saint Francis installed them, with Clare as abbess, as the nucleus of a community in a house by the church of San Damiano. Thus began the order of Poor Ladies, Minoresses, or, simply, Poor Clares.

In 1215, Clare obtained from Pope Innocent III the privilege of poverty, that is, permission for the nuns to live wholly on alms, without possessing any personal or communal property. Their mode of life was harder than that of any other nuns at the time. Such was the nuns' **zeal** for austerity that they did without shoes, slept on the ground, and refrained from eating meat. Clare had to resist attempts at moderation to practice what she called "the most authentic expression of evangelical perfection as understood by Saint Francis of Assisi."

Clare guided her community with discretion for forty years, during which time other houses began throughout Europe. She suffered severe ill health—though she was glimpsed at night tucking in the bedclothes of her nuns. She wrote to a Poor Clare who started a convent in Prague not to overdo her austerities, "for our bodies are not made of brass." She died twenty-seven years after Saint Francis, having left a powerful spiritual legacy in the form of several letters, a rule of life, and, most importantly, her own love for prayer and good works. Greatly revered and respected, credited with many miracles, Clare was declared a saint just two years after she died.

Classics of Christian Spirituality

Certain essential sources, along with Scripture, ought to comprise the "essential spiritual reading" list of every Christian hoping to grow in grace. These include the writings of the Fathers, Doctors, and saints of the church, including **Gregory of Nyssa**, **Bernard of Clairvaux**, **Catherine of Siena**, and **John of the Cross**. Other classics include autobiographical texts such as **Augustine**'s *Confessions* and **Thomas Merton**'s *Sign of Jonas;* treatises written to describe experientially the fundamentals of spiritual life as taught by the Church; and standard texts in the literature of spirituality frequently used by spiritual directors and formation personnel, such as the spiritual letters of **Venerable Francis Libermann** or the conferences of **Vincent de Paul**. Helpful also are biographical texts depicting or explaining the life of Christ, the saints, and the spiritual masters, such as Butler's study of Western mysticism or **Athanasius**' *Life of Saint Antony.*

First-person accounts by people of various faiths can be edifying when they touch reflectively upon aspects of human experience, such as **silence**, **solitude**, having to face suffering and death, discipline, **detachment**, freedom, and so forth. Inspirational value may also be found in novels, plays, poetry, and short fictional works that depict the spiritual nature of men and women as they struggle to find the meaning of life, as they meet their destiny with courage, celebrate creation, and ponder the natural underpinnings of spirituality.

Reading the classics leads us to ponder how much more peaceful we might be if we learned to accept ourselves as God does and to follow his directives from day to day. And as we become more familiar with Holy Scripture and the literature of spirituality, reading the classics proves even more profitable when it is centered in and gathered around fundamental or recurrent themes of spiritual living. The more regular our practice of reading the classics becomes, the more we nourish our spiritual life as a whole.

Clement of Alexandria, Saint

(c. 150-215) This renowned theologian lived at a time of fertile interaction between the Greek and Jewish cultures and the emerging Christian Church. As the director of a Christian school, he accepted the task of bringing Greek philosophy to bear on the interpretation of the Scriptures, thus contradicting the assumption that there was an anti-intellectual bias to Christianity.

Clement saw in the third century, as did **Saint Thomas Aquinas** in the thirteenth, that the Church cannot neglect the findings of pre-Christian philosophy but must see these as servant sources of Christian theology. To objections that "Jerusalem" ought to keep its distance from "Athens," Clement's birthplace, the saint retorted, "Greek philosophy... provides for the soul the preliminary cleansing and training required for the reception of the faith, on which foundation the truth builds up the edifice of knowledge."

Whereas Clement's efforts were more speculative than practical, he succeeded in proving that the message of Christ can best be expounded in minds already prepared by grace to receive it. He resisted any gnostic attempt to subordinate the Gospel to Greek philosophy while affirming the value and beauty of creation, which is after all God's first revelation.

Climacus, John

(d. 649) This master of the contemplative-active life, who came under the influence of both **Evagrius Ponticus** and **John Cassian,** was a hermit monk of the monastery of Saint Catherine on Mount Sinai. Named the most important ascetic theologian of the East, he was chosen abbot of his community and ruled there until shortly before his death. His book, *The Ladder of Divine Ascent* or *The Stairway to Paradise*, a handbook on the ascetic and mystical life, became in the seventh century perhaps the most popular book in the Eastern Church. It was widely used in the West as well and remains an enduring spiritual classic. Its theme of helping souls to practice a life of Christian virtue and to seek at all times and in all ways to attain likeness to God resembles the great work in the Western Church of **Walter Hilton**, who wrote *The Scale of Perfection* in England in the fourteenth century.

Climacus analyzes in thirty chapters or steps (each step representing one year of the hidden life of Jesus of Nazareth) the vices that threaten to deform monks and the virtues that distinguish their life of conformity to Christ. These thirty chapters, which are also reminiscent of the Old Testament patriarch Jacob's dream of the ladder to heaven, describe the steps in the spiritual struggle to moral perfection, a process that culminates in passive **contemplation** and the mystical ecstacy of divine union.

Climacus contrasted not the physical versus the spiritual but the corrupt versus the incorrupt. We must gain through grace the capacity "to distinguish unfailingly between what is truly good and what in nature is opposed to the good."

Our journey to perfection in Christ must be directed by the desire for sanctification of both soul and body. Thus Climacus defines **discernment of spirits** as "a solid understanding of the will of God in all times, in all places, in all things, and it is found among those who are pure in heart, in body, and in speech." The lessons in *The Ladder* indicate that our natural impulses are not corrupt in themselves; rather they have to be redirected toward God in total openness to his commandments with no selfish wants blocking the way. If we are striving upward to reach God, we need never doubt that God is reaching downward to draw us to himself, "for our God," he says, "is a fire consuming all lusts, all stirrings of passion, all predispositions, and all hardness of heart, both within and without, both visible and spiritual."

Cloud of Unknowing, The

(c. 1399) The author of this classical text is an anonymous English monk, whose understanding of the apophatic way comes across in that fresh, earthy, joyful style characteristic of the English spirituality of the fourteenth century. This way of looking negates, so to speak, what we think we know about God so that we can gaze on God with the knowledge of love. The author relies upon a tradition of "negative theology" derived from earlier masterpieces like *The Mystical Theology* by **Pseudo-Dionysius** and the sermons of **Saint Bernard of Clairvaux**, but his own homey yet eloquent style is unmistakable.

The Cloud contains a detailed and practical explanation of **contemplative**

prayer as a gift of grace and an expression of love. The method of **centering prayer** he recommends is similar to the one-word or one-phrase prayer taught by **John Cassian.** Since the way to union with God has to follow the way of negating or forgetting all that is not God, there is a cloud of unknowing which stands between us and God. Thought cannot pierce it, but a "blind stirring" of the will that gives rise to a "sharp dart of longing love" can.

The author further suggests that we press all images, distractions, and memories of past sins and future expectations under the "cloud of forgetting" so that we can enter the "cloud of unknowing," desiring God for his own sake, not for his gifts but for his gracious being. We are to center our attention on him, letting both wonder and worry fade into forgetting. What counts most is our "naked intent" toward God, a movement of our will to be united with him in the depths of our heart. We have to learn to be at home in this darkness, illumined only by a flame of **faith** that asks nothing of God but God himself. We are to return to this "ray of darkness" as often as we can, for in it dwells our entire good, who is God ineffable, merciful, eter-

Come, Spirit of Love

Spirit of consolation, unfailing source of joy and peace,
Inspire solidarity with the poor,
Grant the sick the strength they need,
Pour out trust and hope upon those experiencing trials,
Awaken in all hearts a commitment to a better future.
Come, Spirit of love and peace!

Spirit of wisdom, inspiration of minds and hearts,
Direct science and technology
To the service of life, justice and peace.
Render fruitful our dialogue with the followers of other religions,
Lead the different cultures to appreciate the values of the Gospel.
Spirit of life, by whose power the Word was made flesh
In the womb of the Virgin Mary, the woman of attentive silence,
Make us docile to the promptings of your love
And ever ready to accept the signs of the times
Which you place along the paths of history.
Come, Spirit of love and peace!

To you, Spirit of love,
With the Almighty Father and the Only-Begotten Son,
Be praise, honor and glory
Forever and ever. Amen

–Pope John Paul II

nally in love with humankind.

As we experience absorption in **contemplative prayer**, we become more attentive to the voice of conscience. Sin is experienced as a "lump," a useless, heavy burden pulling us away from our center. We seek friendship with God by coming to know and love the truth that we are only servants. In the author's body of work, reading, thinking, and praying are seen as one and the same activity, for the soul cannot move toward the higher stages of **contemplation** without humbly attending to the Word of God. Thus he says: "So I want you to understand clearly that for beginners and those a little advanced in contemplation, reading or hearing the word of God must precede pondering it and without time given to serious reflection there will be no genuine prayer."

Communion of Saints

Both in the Apostles' Creed and in the Nicene Creed, we express our belief in this assembly of the saints as one of the essentials of the Christian faith. Quoting **Saint Thomas Aquinas**, the *Catechism* states: "Since all the faithful form one body, the good of each is communicated to the others" [947][2]. As Christ is the head of the Church, so are his riches communicated to the members through the sacraments, above all, the **Eucharist**.

According to the *Catechism*, two meanings are in this one phrase: communion "in holy things" and "among holy persons" [948]. This *sanctorum communio* helps to explain what Paul means in 1 Corinthians 12:26, when he says, speaking of the Mystical Body of Christ, that "If [one] part suffers, all the parts suffer with it; if one part is honored, all the parts share its joy."

This beautiful vision of solidarity, which extends not only to the living but also to the dead, to the souls in purgatory and in heaven, is an expression of our celebration of the communion of saints. As our faith teaches, "... the least of our acts done in charity redounds to the profit of all" and, by the same token, "every sin harms this communion" [953]. Just as Christian communion (fellowship on earth) brings us closer to one another, "so our communion with the saints joins us to Christ, from whom as from its fountain and head issues all grace, and the life of the People of God itself" [957][3].

Compassion

The Latin roots of this word are *cum* (with) and *passio* (to suffer), suggesting that compassion means to suffer empathetically with our own and others' vulnerability. As bearers of Christ in the world we are called to show compassion for all people—family members and friends, rich and poor, those who share our **faith** tradition and those who adhere to other belief systems. It is a question not only of being compassionate with people in general but of showing genuine compassion in specific situations with suffering persons, with the vulnerability of a life that misses the mark, due perhaps to illness, injustice, conflict, or defeat.

Compassion suggests in the same vein that we remain as sensitive to our own vulnerability as to that of others. Sensing our limits helps us to avoid a style of care that would hurt or humiliate people who seem to have less than we do. Any form of condescending care violates the disposition of appreciating our own and others' dependency on a power greater than we. Judgmentalism also paralyzes Christian compassion. The more we come to know one another with our failings and vulnerabilities, the more we realize how profound is our need for understanding and **forgiveness**. A marvelous example of nonjudgmental compassion can be found in the following account from the sayings of the **Desert Fathers:**

> A brother at Scetis committed a fault. A council was called to which Abba Moses was invited, but he refused to go to it. Then the priest sent someone to say to him, "Come, for everyone is waiting for you." So he got up and went. He took a leaking jug, filled it with water, and carried it with him. The others came out to meet him and said to him, "What is this, Father?" The old man said to them, "My sins run out behind me, and I do not see them, and today I am coming to judge the errors of another." When they heard that they said no more to the brother but forgave him.

Compunction

In the Christian East an entire doctrine is built around the disposition of *penthos* or compunction. It refers to the riveting awareness that we are sinners in need of redemption. It is like a wake-up call that comes over us Christians when we realize that our sins sever us from the fullness of God's presence. *Penthos* is not morbid self-guilt or masochistic "breast-beating." It is godly sorrow. It is true repentance. It is regret for any self-centered choice that has separated us from God and deprived us of the joy of his **forgiveness**.

Accompanying *penthos* is often the gift of tears caused by the commingling of genuine contrition for sin and equally profound gratitude for reconciliation. Though comfort comes through compunction, we can never grow complacent or stop repenting of our sins until the Lord himself sees fit "to wipe away every tear from [our] eyes" (Revelation 7:17). The Fathers believe that *penthos* is not something we do; it is an act of God in us, awakening us to the truth of who we are. Hence the outcome of perpetual compunction is said to be unending happiness rooted in the remembrance of God's saving grace.

Compunction, from the Latin *cumpungere*, is likened to a shock, a sting, a blow, or a sort of burning. God presses us with insistence toward the pursuit of new life in him, lest we be dulled into complacency by worldly comforts devoid of deeper meaning. *Penthos* is a gift beyond our power to control. It represents the start of a "second **conversion**" by which grace forms in us a new spiritual sensitivity to all that God wants and allows. For example, Jesus could not reach the Samaritan woman until she experienced compunction of heart (John 4:4-29). Compunction "hollows out" self-centeredness and increases our capacity for God.

Thomas à Kempis offers us wise counsel in *The Imitation of Christ*, when he says of this experience, "I would rather feel compunction of heart for my sins than merely know the definition of compunction." What we do know is that there can be no true discipleship without it.

Confirmation

To complete the grace of **Baptism**, Christians need to receive the sacrament of Confirmation, for through it the Holy Spirit strengthens our **faith**, deepens our love and our loyalty to the Church, and helps us to be witnesses to Christ's way in the world. According to the *Catechism*, the very name "Christian" means "anointed" [1289]. This sacrament endows us with special strength so that we can both spread and defend the faith as true witnesses of Christ. It signifies in a new way that we are children of God and heirs of heaven. It is through the Spirit that we receive the virtues and gifts that enable us to make a renewed commitment to Christian action.

The essential rite of Confirmation in the Roman Catholic Church consists of the anointing with chrism on one's forehead, which is done by the laying on of hands and through the words the bishop speaks: "Be sealed with the Gift of the Holy Spirit" [1300][4]. The sign of **peace** shared at the conclusion of the sacrament signifies that between the bishop and all the faithful there is a bond of unity, an "ecclesial communion" [1301], whose wondrous effects we ought to feel over a lifetime.

The parish, like the family, is responsible for preparing young people and adults for Confirmation. To receive this holy sacrament, one has to be in a state of grace. One ought, therefore, to receive the sacrament of Penance prior to its bestowal [1309-1310]. For Confirmation one has also to seek the spiritual support of a sponsor, who ideally ought to be one of one's baptismal godparents [1311]. It is the bishop who ministers this sacrament ordinarily in the Latin rite. By conferring Confirmation himself, the bishop "demonstrates clearly that its effect is to unite those who receive it more closely to the Church, to her apostolic origins, and to her mission of bearing witness to Christ" [1313]. Only under grave circumstances, for instance, if a Christian is in danger of death, can a priest be the minister of Confirmation. The reason for this is that "the Church desires that none of her children, even the youngest, should depart this world without having been perfected by the Holy Spirit with the gift of Christ's fullness" [1314], to be embodied in a variety of states of life and in accordance with a diversity of talents and skills.

Consolations

Consolations are spiritual blessings or various other communications from God to us, which ought to evoke our gratitude and rekindle the disposition of awe without themselves becoming the object of our desire. Saint Luke tells us in his Gospel about the righteous and devout man, Simeon, who was "awaiting the consolation of Israel" (Luke 2:25). The Holy Spirit had promised Simeon that before his death he would see the Messiah of Israel. When he took the child Jesus in his arms, he was both awed and consoled. His old eyes beheld the Supreme Consolation prepared by the Father for the glory of his people.

Not only does God console us in sorrow and grant us touches of joy. He encourages us to be sources of comfort and consolation to one another as a means of strengthening our **faith** (Romans 1:12), especially in times of trial and **desolation**. The warm, loving, peaceful "showings" of God, his unsolicited and undeserved visitations, evoke in recipients a wide range of emotions: tears of joy and sorrow for sin, a longing for the life to come when we shall be "filled with all the fullness of God" (Ephesians 3:19), and a desire for **conversion**.

Saint Ignatius of Loyola offers excellent counsel in the *Spiritual Exercises* by which we can distinguish essential consolation or "substantial **devotion**" from transitory feelings. If a consolation comes to us directly from God, without any previous cause or even known merit on our part, our response must be a deeper commitment to do God's will and his work, despite the fluctuations of feeling we may experience. We also need to know that God may send us the grace of consolation in the earlier stages of the spiritual journey to encourage our progress and to strengthen our faith, provided we keep in mind the difference between the consolations of God and the God who consoles.

Contemplation

To contemplate means literally to be in the temple of the living God, sensing, believing, and experiencing that we are actually in his presence, that he is in us and we are in him. Cooperating with this grace means letting go of prideful, rebellious, selfish tendencies. We let God's **peace** expand and penetrate our hearts and minds. We strive to obey God's commandments, to flow with the teachings and traditions of the Church, to live up to our commitments, but we do all of these things out of an inner motivation to temper our ego so thoroughly that it is no longer we who live, but Christ who lives in us (Galatians 2:20). Our whole life becomes oriented to God. **Contemplation** is the final fruit of **Baptism**, not the privilege of an elite few but a grace available to all.

Contemplation is "acquired" if the acts associated with **contemplative prayer** are the results of our good will and graced efforts; it is "infused" if these acts, produced by divine grace, happen without, or nearly without, any human effort at all. Whatever the case may be, we begin to live in **humility, detachment**, and **charity**, virtues that, according to **Saint Teresa of Avila,** are sure and essential companions of contemplation.

One sign that we are on the way may come paradoxically in the form of dryness or **aridity**. The process by which God purifies our sensual and spiritual desires is bound at times to be painful. Yet the new lights he allows to glow in our soul can only be fully appreciated against the background of dark and dry self-stripping. To the contemplative, God is a ray of darkness, a wonder unspeakable, an incomprehensible mystery beyond us and yet intimately near to us. The contemplative experience is admittedly paradoxical. Though of short duration, its effects are lasting.

Contemplative Prayer

Seeking God in pure **faith, hope**, and love, focused solely on him no matter how distracted, dry, or discouraged we may feel, is a sure avenue to contemplative prayer. We strive to adore God with praise and thanksgiving in whatever state we find ourselves. The *Catechism* compares contemplative prayer to what it is like to enter into the Eucharistic liturgy: "We 'gather up' the heart, recollect our whole being under the prompting of the Holy Spirit, abide in the dwelling place of the Lord which we are, awaken our faith in order to enter into the presence of him who awaits us" [2711].

In contemplative prayer we do not need to hide anything from God. He loves us, and we love him. He sees us, and we see him, taking off our masks and turning to him with all our heart, asking him to purify and transform us. In **humility** and **poverty of spirit**, we surrender our wills to the Father in union with his beloved Son. The *Catechism* reminds us that contemplative prayer is not our doing; it is a gift and grace of God, a covenant relationship, a communion with the **Blessed Trinity** [2713].

To contemplate the mystery of love operable in our lives and in the world is to participate in the "yes" of Jesus to the Father, in the *"fiat"* of the **Blessed Virgin Mary** to the Holy Spirit. Such love is never self-contained; it gives life to the world. It passes through the night of Jesus' agony in the garden, his paschal sacrifice on the cross, his burial in the tomb, and on to the bright morn of his resurrected glory. As **Henri J.M. Nouwen** puts it: "In contemplative prayer, Christ cannot remain a stranger who lived long ago in a foreign world. Rather, he becomes a living presence with whom we can enter into dialogue here and now."

Conversion

Conversion means radical rejection of sin and an intentional turn or return (*metanoia*) to God. It is not a *yes* said once and for all but a complete reformation or redirection of one's life. Different from our first conversion in **Baptism** is the experience some Christians have of a "second conversion" or personal pledge of their entire life to the love and service of God. If the first Baptism is of water, then the second is often of tears. Some conversions are hardly noticeable. Others, like that of Saint Paul on the road to Damascus or **Saint Augustine** in the garden or **Saint Ignatius of Loyola** on his sickbed, are dramatic and intense, involving the transformation of one's entire life and world.

At the core of the evangelization process is the call to conversion to those who as yet do not know Christ or his teachings. Just as **faith** is a gift, so conversion is the graced movement of a "contrite heart" (Psalm 51:17), responding to the merciful love of God. That explains why it is often impossible to separate conversion from repentance and reconciliation. It is at the core of interior conversion that lasting transformation of the heart takes place. Only at the level of the love-will can we choose to conform our lives to Christ, reject evil, and turn away from personal and social sin.

As we read in the *Catechism*, this conversion is never facile or exterior only. Accompanying it is "a salutary pain and sadness which the Fathers called *animi cruciatus* (affliction of spirit) and *compunctio cordis* (repentance of heart)" [1431].[5] We must be eternally grateful to God for the grace he gives us to begin anew despite the frailty and false starts that may have characterized our lives up to that time. The blessings of conversion far outweigh the risks inherent in one's definite *yes* to God. Through this turning we discover not only the greatness of God's love but also the capacity he gives us to do great things in his name.

Cyprian of Carthage, Saint

(c. 200-258) A man of God equally loved by pagans and Christians, Cyprian, as bishop of Carthage, wrote a number of letters offering penetrating insights into the affairs of the Church in Africa in the middle of the third century. This was a period of crisis and persecution. Threats of a schism were the worst fruits of the scandalous dissensions among Christians of his day. Problems of doctrine and discipline had to be addressed to members of a **faith** in its infancy, who, like Cyprian himself, had only one end awaiting them—martyrdom.

Cyprian tackled these weighty issues with gentleness and firmness, moderation and courage, and a manifest love for the Word of God. As a bishop, he knew himself to be directly responsible to God for his actions. The theme of the various councils he guided was unity, not division, the imitation of Christ, never expediency, judgmentalism, or lack of perseverance. He put upon himself and his clergy the commitment to set a good example by seeking reconciliation with the Church, an increase of faith, and the worthy reception of the **Eucharist**. In one of his own letters, he gave a fitting summary of his life: "He cannot have God for his Father who does not have the Church for his Mother."

Cyril of Jerusalem, Saint

(c. 315-s86) As bishop of the Holy City, Cyril attended the First Council of Constantinople in 381 and authored a series of catechetical lectures to defend the true divinity of Christ. In a time marked by more than one heresy, he never wavered in his orthodoxy, especially when it came to combating **Arianism**. He contends: "For not according to men's pleasure have the articles of **faith** been composed, but the most important points collected from the Scriptures make up one complete teaching of the faith. And just as the mustard seed in a small grain contains in embryo many future branches, so also the creed embraces in a few words all the religious knowledge in both the Old and the New Testament."

Commemorated among the blessed in the Eastern Church since the fifth century and named by Pope Leo XIII as a Doctor of the universal Church, Cyril stands in the forefront of spiritual theologians favorable to the "way of negation," the insistence that we can know of God only what has been revealed in a divine, transcendent manner. Cyril believed that the purpose of this revelation was to guide our worship to its proper end, this being **devotion** and good conduct.

1. cf. CIC, can. 713 § 2.
2. St. Thomas Aquinas, § 10.
3. LG 50, cf. Eph 4:1-6.
4. Paul VI, apostolic constitution, *Divinae consortium naturae,* 663.
5. cf. Council of Trent (1551): DS 1676-1678; 1705; cf. *Roman Catechism,* II, V, 4.

Dark Night of the Soul

By using the imagery of the "night," **Saint John of the Cross** describes with the help of a powerful metaphor that part of our spiritual journey in which deprivations of worldly powers, pleasures, and possessions tempt us to think we may have been abandoned by God. (See **Desolations** and **Purgative Way.**) And yet the opposite is true. As we begin to mortify these attachments, we may be drawn by grace to a new sense of God's presence even in his seeming absence. We are led still deeper into the night—to the midnight hour where the only proximate means of union is pure **faith**.

Through the nights of sense and spirit, both active and passive, God allows us to discover that no thing, concept, image, or idea can fulfill our infinite desire for union with him. As our appetites are purged in the "active night of sense," a more intense love of God is enkindled in us. However, since sensory appetites are always in a state of "craving," our spiritual faculties (intellect, memory, and will) must be purified in the "active night of the spirit" by an increase, respectively, of faith, **hope**, and love. When the house of willful appetites is stilled through the mortification of sensuality, the soul is free to move with a lighter step toward union with the Beloved. For this reason Saint John can proclaim that renunciation is but a stage on the way to lasting liberation.

The soul also has to undergo a still deeper transformation in the passive nights of sense and spirit to rid itself of the life-draining parasites of inordinate spiritual appetites like pride and avarice, envy and sloth, which cause us to live and act as if we were in control of our destiny. The dark night disrupts this delusion. It plunges us into the unknown land of contemplative openness to the "More Than," to the mystery of being and nonbeing no rational mind can fathom. Only faith can give meaning to this mystery. To believe is to allow the initiative for final decision and action to shift from us to God. The center of gravity then becomes not self-survival but self-surrender.

At these times of maximum receptivity, when the initiative for union belongs wholly to God, what is a soul to do? How ought we to conduct ourselves? Saint John offers wise counsel in this regard. We derive from reading his works that: (1) Rather than feeling confused, we ought to feel comforted, as though we were children clasping the hands of our parents in a swirling crowd. As long as we hold tight, we cannot get lost. (2) Rather than succumbing to the temptation to return to more comfortable quarters, we must persevere patiently, wait upon the Lord, and ponder in prayer if discomforts and afflictions are perhaps blessings in disguise, invitations to deepen our faith, calls for conversion of heart. (3) Instead of trusting our own urgings to regain control, we must place our trust in God, as a sick child trusts his or her parents to administer proper medicine. Then we can see, even in these midnight moments, that ours is a God of infinite love, who meets the needs of sincere seekers, who walk the way of the cross, as Jesus did, with unflinching courage and unending love.

Day of Judgment

Surely, when the day of judgment comes we shall not be asked what we have read but what we have done, not how well we have spoken but how devoutly we have lived.

–Thomas à Kempis

Day, Dorothy

(1897-1980) A native of New York, Day returned to the city after living in California and studying in Chicago, to work as a reporter for a socialist newspaper. It was in her daily confrontation with the relentless **poverty** of tenement dwellers that she came to see her call to serve the poor.

Feeling drawn to God after the birth of her daughter, Day was baptized a Catholic. From then on, she maintained a lifelong **devotion** to the **Eucharist**. Following her **conversion,** she separated from her common-law husband and stayed on with her daughter in New York, seeking further direction for her life. It was in New York that she met Peter Maurin (1877-1949), with whom she founded the Catholic Worker movement in the immigrant neighborhoods of New York's Lower East Side. The two opened a house of hospitality that gave credence and concreteness to the corporal works of **mercy**: feeding the hungry, clothing the naked, sheltering the homeless.

The aims of the movement, in addition to personalist action, were voluntary poverty, a commitment to human rights, and pacifism or Gospel nonviolence. She and Peter began a newspaper, now sent to subscribers worldwide, at the price, which has never changed, of a penny a copy. A gifted writer, her autobiography, *The Long Loneliness,* is considered a twentieth-century classic, reflecting the depth of her own "yearning toward God."

De Caussade, Jean-Pierre

(1675-1751) This renowned director of souls was a member of the Society of Jesus, which he entered at Toulouse in 1693. Throughout his life, de Caussade displayed gifts of teaching and preaching, albeit in a hidden manner. An outstanding confessor and spiritual counselor, he gave conferences over many years to the nuns of the Order of the Visitation at Nancy and undertook to direct several members. The sisters preserved his conference notes and extensive correspondence, but they remained unpublished for many years. In 1861, his writings found their way into print under the title *Abandonment to Divine Providence*, a book now regarded as a spiritual classic.

De Caussade spoke of each passing moment as being not only "the veil of God" but also, when scrutinized and interpreted by **faith**, "the unveiling of God." He gave the term "sacrament of the present moment" to this understanding of time pierced by the Eternal. As he understood it, duties, temptations, and trials are shadows that hide the action of the Divine Will in the treasure of the ordinary, in the here and now of daily life. For him, the Christian life is both an active and a passive cooperation with God, moment by moment. The kind of prayer he recommended for everyone was a simple waiting upon God to discern his presence and to do his will.

De Caussade did publish one book in his lifetime, in 1741, titled *On Prayer*, comprised of a set of dialogues on the art and discipline of **contemplative living**. According to this experienced director of souls, the aim of prayer is to lead one toward the practice of simple recollection and attention to God. De Caussade showed little interest in exceptional states of prayer or in complex analyses of the route to perfection. The key to spiritual maturity, he insisted, resides not in self-seeking but in self-giving. Consequently, complete surrender to the **will of God** is the essence of spirituality and the supreme duty of souls, for "the great and firm foundation of the spiritual life is the offering of ourselves to God and being subject to his will in all things."

Once we have this foundation, we come to understand that, in the hands of God, misfortune, illness, spiritual weakness—all bear fruit and turn into what is good for us. Such happenings are the disguises God assumes so we may reach that pure faith, which enables us to recognize him under any appearance. How consoling it is to know, in the words of de Caussade, that "the realization that God is active in all that happens at every moment is the deepest knowledge we can have in this life of the things of God."

De Foucauld, Charles

(1858-1916) As a youth, Charles was the last person one could ever imagine entering religious life, becoming a Little Brother of Jesus, and dying a martyr's death. Born into a highly placed, wealthy family from Strasbourg, he sought to make a career for himself in the military. This avocation proved to be a disaster. He was so spoiled and weak of character that not even the army wanted him. Though born and baptized into the Catholic faith, he declared himself to be an agnostic, a posture that may have given him the excuse he needed to lead a hedonistic lifestyle.

While Charles was in the military, he did discover the desert of North Africa, a geographical wonder that would strangely enough prove to be his destiny. On an expedition there, he observed the piety of the Muslim community and began, by contrast, to question the shallowness of his own life.

On Christmas Day, 1886, he made his confession in a Paris church, became a convert to the **faith** he had denied, and rigorously gave his life to Jesus. He chose to enter the Trappists as a brother in a monastery in Syria, where he could imitate as closely as possible the hidden life of Nazareth. Having sought ordination, he felt the call to return to the desert region bordering Morocco, to an oasis named Béni-Abbes. His dream was to develop a new community of brothers whose life would proclaim the gospel through acts of service.

On Pentecost Sunday, June 6, 1897, the Lord communicated to Charles what was to be the essence of his vocation. For the next fifteen years he modeled the rule of **solitude** he wished for his community, believing that from it would come the fruit of solidarity. Rather than trying to cope with the increasing congestion in his surroundings, he sought and found a more remote desert hermitage in Tamanrasset, but it was to be his final move. On December 1, 1916, he was the victim of a violent death at the hands of Tuareg rebels, experiencing to the full the prayer of **abandonment to Divine Providence** that would become his legacy.

De Montfort, Saint Louis-Marie Grignion

(1673-1716) Vagabond preacher, troubadour, and artist, De Montfort became a mystic who served the poorest of the poor in France as the pope's "apostolic missionary" until his death. While he was still a seminarian, he taught catechism to rough street urchins in Paris. After he was ordained in 1700, he served as a hospital chaplain, as a minister to the sick and a caregiver for the homeless, unwed mothers, and other outcasts of society. In 1703 he wrote his most significant theological book, *The Love of Eternal Wisdom*, and organized the Daughters of Wisdom, the first of three religious congregations inspired by his teaching and example, the other two being the Company of Mary and the Brothers of Saint Gabriel.

A student and follower of the **French School of Spirituality**, De Montfort was a lover of the cross of Christ. His chief **charism** was to spearhead a still growing, worldwide movement of consecration to God alone through the **Blessed Virgin Mary**. Pope John Paul II is an excellent example of the continuing influence of De Montfort, for from him he borrowed his motto, *Totus Tuus* ("All Yours"). This motto reflects the saint's emphasis on the primacy of God and on our need to abandon ourselves to his will in all things.

Saint Louis traveled thousands of miles, mostly by foot, to preach missions and to call people to reform their lives by conforming them more to Jesus and Mary. Often the brunt of jealousy and misunderstanding, he chose to return love for dislike. In 1712 he wrote the book for which he is still famous, *Treatise on the True Devotion to the Blessed Virgin*. It has been called *the* western classic on Marian spirituality and consecration. Saint Louis died as he would have wished: preaching from the pulpit on **conversion** of heart.

Desert Experience

The desert is first of all a physical place, usually associated with hot sun, dry sand and dust, sparse vegetation. From earliest times, within and outside of Christianity, it has been a place to which people retreated when they sought intense **solitude**, **silence**, and closeness to God. Secondly, desert is another word for place of spiritual retreat. This place can be the geographical desert, but it can also be a retreat center, a hermit's dwelling, or a house of prayer. Thirdly, desert refers to an inner experience of **detachment** and letting go. In the desert of the heart one learns the true meaning of life.

The desert theme appears throughout the Old and New Testaments, whether we recall the experience of the Israelites moving toward the Promised Land or the preparatory forty days of our Lord prior to beginning his public life. For the chosen people, the desert experience was God's means of readying them for a more intimate encounter with him.

The desert is a great teacher. Like soldiers who have trained long and hard to carry out a difficult mission, so Jesus' disciples must go through desert training, disciplining pride and its desperate clinging to power, pleasure, and possession. In the desert we learn to wait upon the Lord and to listen to his will in our daily situation. The desperation we feel in our personal desert moments should not give way to discouragement or despair. These experiences teach us that failures and imperfections are not insurmountable obstacles to God; paradoxically they are conditions for the possibility of enjoying true intimacy.

Desert Fathers

In the fourth century A.D., a group of holy men and women (abbas and ammas) from the remote regions of Egypt, Syria, and Palestine brought to life a body of oral and written sayings and tributes, narratives and counsels that inspired and continue to inspire believers seeking a closer relationship with God. Written in languages like Coptic, Syriac, Greek, and Latin, this "literature of the desert" formed a genre in its own right, the humor and **humility** of which is timeless.

A certain Abba Agathon, for example, once met a cripple on the roadside, who asked him where he was going. When he was told Agathon's destination, he boldly asked the old man to carry him there, which he gladly did. But that was not the end of the story. Soon after the two of them arrived in town, the cripple said to him, "Put me down where you sell your wares." Agathon did so and went to work. No sooner had he sold an article than the cripple asked, "What did you sell it for?" and he told him the price. At that the man insisted Agathon buy him a cake, which he did. Then the Abba sold a second article. Again the sick man asked, "How much did you sell it for?", and he was told the price. He then asked Agathon to buy him something else, and he obliged. At sunset, when all this selling and buying had come to an end, Agathon, tired as he was, was asked by the man to do him a favor and carry him back to the place where he had been at the start of the day. Once more picking him up, Agathon carried him back to the exact spot. Then the cripple said, "Agathon, you are filled with divine blessings, in heaven and on earth." Raising his eyes, Agathon saw no man; it was an **angel** of the Lord, come to try him.

Some of the best known and loved of the Desert Fathers and Mothers include, among others, **Saint Antony of Egypt,** Arsenius, Theodore of Pherme, Theodora, John the Dwarf, Macarius the Great, Moses, Poemen (called the Shepherd), Sarah, **John Cassian**, and **Evagrius Ponticus.** These great-spirited Christians all placed a high value on **asceticism** as the only trustworthy basis for **mysticism**. They could never be content with speculation about God; they sought experiential knowledge of his love, compassion, friendship, and perfection.

Desolations

Being led by God into the desert of deprivation, devoid of consolation, can be a terrifying experience, a true **dark night of the soul**, in which we undergo the inner stripping that can ready us for a life of **contemplation**.

Desolation shakes our complacency to the core. What previously required little effort on our part now demands tiring labor. We struggle to pray, to meditate, to do **spiritual reading**, but we have to press on in pure faith. Dryness displaces delight, **aridity** all previous awakenings. We must not confuse this spiritual movement with lukewarmness or tepidity, for it has a definite purpose. What is happening can confuse us, even depress us, unless we realize that this experience offers us a chance to grow in self-knowledge and spiritual maturity.

Desolation, properly understood, ought not to be a source of discouragement but an occasion, offered by God, to liberate us from the domination of pride and vainglory. It opens us to receive infused graces. Best of all, we learn not to rely on whatever sensible consolations we derive from our spiritual exercises. With the equanimity of the man Job we learn to say, "The LORD gave and the LORD has taken away; /blessed be the name of the LORD" (Job 1:21). What matters is neither desolation nor consolation, only that we move in the direction God wants us to go.

Detachment

Spiritual masters agree that this disposition is an essential condition for the possibility of living a Christ-centered life of love and **humility**. Detachment is like preventive medicine for the soul. It protects us from inordinate attachments to power, pleasure, and possession. It puts Christ, not lesser goods or selfish motivations, at the center of our concerns.

Detachment must not be misunderstood as a matter of negating what is good or God-given but as the graced capacity to let go of any person, event, or thing as ultimate or as more important than God. Detachment redirects us away from self-aggrandizement and toward the glory of God. In other words, detachment is not only a matter of relegating possessions to their proper place; it also challenges us to accept that in the end we possess nothing at all and that everything is God's gift.

In *The Way of Perfection*, **Saint**

Teresa of Avila helps us to see the positive side of detachment. She tells her sisters that if this virtue is "practiced with perfection, [it] includes everything." Once God alone becomes the source and goal of our lives, nothing—no amount of status, honor, fame, or wealth—can exclude him or separate us from his love. The solution for the detached heart is not to despise creation but to embrace the Creator. In this way we come to see all that is in relation to the One in whom and through whom everything exists in the first place.

In addition to maintaining this inner stance of respectful distance with regard to material possessions, we must also detach ourselves from interior clutter, from images and ideas that count more for us than **abandonment to Divine Providence.** Saint Teresa calls this inner work the real labor of detachment. It may mean disentangling ourselves from bodily comforts that lead to disobedience; avoiding heroic penances that lack discretion and increase vanity; practicing **silence**; ceasing to complain about slight sicknesses. In this way, we begin to practice the "long martyrdom" of interior mortification that empties us of self so that we may be full of God.

Devils

In Sacred Scripture there are many references to demons or devils or evil spirits, though it is clear that the power of Satan can never surpass the sovereign power of God. Nonetheless, Scripture has it that Satan and his cohorts can wield power over humans weakened by original sin. Unlike the **angels** of God who work for our benefit, the devils are bent on our destruction. Having rebelled against God, these once angelic spirits lost supernatural grace. Along with Satan or Lucifer, their leader, they were condemned to hell.

According to the *Catechism*, this "fall" of the angels "consists in the free choice of these created spirits, who radically and irrevocably *rejected* God and his reign" [392]. Therefore, behind the choice to disobey God, made by our first parents, there "lurks a seductive voice, opposed to God, which makes them fall into death out of envy" [391].[1] As we read in the Book of Revelation, "The huge dragon, the ancient serpent, who is called the devil and Satan, who deceived the whole world, was thrown down to earth, and its angels were thrown down with it" (Revelation 12:9).

This act of disobedience was so defiant, so unrepentant, as to be irrevocable. Its disastrous influence explains why these fallen spirits became the archenemies of God and man. Jesus describes the devil as "a murderer from the beginning" in whom there is no truth "because he is a liar and the father of lies" (John 8:44). His full fury was unleashed on the day God revealed that a Savior would come to redeem us humans from sin. Satan directed all his energy from that time forward to defeat this divine purpose and to exercise his power over us, but it is not infinite. As the *Catechism* reminds us, the devil "is only a creature, powerful from the fact that he is a pure spirit, but still a creature. He cannot prevent the building up of God's reign" [395]. In the **Lord's Prayer**, we ask God to deliver us from evil, but this prayer is only possible because we believe with the whole Church that Christ Jesus has already won the victory over the "ruler of this world" [2864].

Devotio Moderna

This "modern devotional" or "new devotion" movement began in the Netherlands in the fourteenth century when an interest in the mystical life, prayer, **meditation**, and piety swept across the continent. In the same century we witness, for example, the rise of the English school of Spirituality, with such notable figures as the anonymous author of ***The Cloud of Unknowing***, **Walter Hilton**, **Julian of Norwich**, and **Richard Rolle**.

Devotio moderna soon spread throughout the Rhineland and into France, Germany, Italy, and Spain. Its main proponents were the Brothers of the Common Life and the Canons Regular of **Saint Augustine**. These pious souls embraced a life of **poverty**, **chastity**, and **obedience** on a voluntary basis rather than under monastic vows, devoting their lives to the service of God in the world.

The movement, though affecting religious life, was largely oriented toward the spiritual life of laity in the world, who had to face and combat purely humanistic values. At its center stood the person of Jesus Christ, the gospel, and works on his life written in the **Cistercian** and **Franciscan** traditions. The founder of the modern devotion was a canon lawyer and writer named Master Geert Groote (1340-84). Following a **conversion** experience in 1374, he abandoned his legal career, opened his home to a group of women (the Sisters of the Common Life), and sought a period of monastic **solitude** as preparation for his life as a preacher and spiritual director.

Perhaps the best-known book the movement produced, a text still widely read and venerated today as the most influential devotional book in the history of Western Christianity, is *The Imitation of Christ* by **Thomas à Kempis**. In it one finds a characteristic emphasis on affective **devotion** and contemplative affinity to the humanity of Jesus. *The Imitation* shows that from union with the **will of God** there flows naturally communion with others for his sake. To renounce what is vain and seek what is humble, one must follow the Crucified Christ.

In this way, the movement set forth the principles by which any sincere Christian could live a deeper spiritual life in conformity to Christ and with **humility**. While as a movement the "new devotion" was absorbed by the revival of religious life in the sixteenth century and by the Reformation as such, its fruits remain in the emphasis the Church places on the universal **call to holiness** and on a Eucharistic and Christ-centered **mysticism**.

Devotion

Praying the rosary, venerating icons, choosing patron saints, participating in processions on holy days, making the stations of the cross, going on a pilgrimage to sacred places—all of these symbols, images, and acts are expressions of personal and communal devotion. This word is derived from the Latin, *devovere*, meaning to give oneself over to someone or something out of fervent conviction. It follows that those who receive the grace of a sincere spiritual life subject themselves to the Divine Will and to whatever concerns the service of God.

Devotion becomes a disposition that permeates one's life as a whole. It is like the soil in which the spiritual exercises, stemming from liturgy, word, and sacrament, can bud and flower. It suggests an openness to the Sacred that makes one eager to practice **silence, spiritual reading, meditation**, prayer, **contemplation**, and Christian action. All these spiritual disciplines presuppose the need for purification from self-centeredness.

Devotions not only redirect our energy toward what is good and holy; they also dispose us to foster an inner climate of receptivity to divine guidance. They are to be understood not as privatized expressions of piety but as pointers to the highest goal of union with God. Devotions are neither goals in their own right nor guarantors of salvation. We do not practice devotions to gain holiness by any effort of our own but to listen more intently to what God asks of us. As Scripture says, "Train yourself for devotion, for, while physical training is of limited value, devotion is valuable in every respect, since it holds a promise of life both for the present and for the future" (1 Timothy 4:7-8).

Discernment of Spirits

This biblical **charism** is named by Saint Paul in his First Epistle to the Corinthians (12:10), and it has a longstanding tradition in the writings of the Greek and Latin Church Fathers and spiritual masters, who place a high value on the virtue of *discretio spirituum* or, simply, discretion. What it means is that one has or cultivates the graced ability to discern the presence or absence of God. Is it his Spirit or some other spirit that is guiding human actions? Is one or is one not living in fidelity to the **will of God**?

These "spirits" embody themselves in our human affections as well as in our actions. They need to be appraised by us but also by wise and prudent spiritual guides. In all cases, they must respond to the Gospel directive, "By their fruits you will know them" (Matthew 7:16).

This charism operates on that inner battlefield where we must discern if the spirit moving us is of God or of the **devil**; if, in more modern terms, we are being prompted from within by a genuine call or perhaps entangled in any number of psychological aberrations ranging from the hysterical to the compulsive.

In many ways, discernment is more an art than a discipline. Great practitioners of discretion like the **Desert Fathers**, **John Cassian**, and **John Climacus** had the capacity to read the heart of a disciple and to know under what spirit one acted. Their fragmentary wisdom and anecdotal illustrations gained a much needed systematic framework when **Saint Ignatius of Loyola** wrote his *Spiritual Exercises.* He designed these to be a manual for retreat directors to help them understand the different movements produced in the soul so that one could admit what was of God and reject what was of the world, the flesh, and the **devil**.

Distractions in Prayer

The *Catechism* identifies distraction as "the habitual difficulty in prayer" [2729]. It can affect **vocal prayer**, be it liturgical or personal, as well as mental and **contemplative prayer**, disrupting inner **peace** and concentrated presence to God.

When we are distracted, it is generally best not to battle the distractions directly. If we do, then it is likely that we will be in double trouble—distracted by our distractions! As the *Catechism* counsels, "To set about hunting down distractions would be to fall into their trap, when all that is necessary is to turn back to our heart" [2729].

Even our distractions can be put to spiritual benefit, however; they may cause us to reappraise that to which we are inordinately attached—be it a person, event, or thing, an image or an idea, a plan or a project. We can then at least ponder if it has become more important to us than God and if that is why we are so distracted by it.

Once we grow in the humble awareness that such a distraction may be the sign of an excessive attachment, we can return to the Lord and reawaken "our preferential love for him" while at the same time renewing our resolution "to offer him our heart to be purified" [2729]. The questions posed by distractions in prayer are these: What master do we want to serve (Matthew 6:24)? Where is our heart (Matthew 6:21)?

The disposition that counters distractions is not forced attention to them but gentle vigilance or "sobriety of heart" [2730]. When distractions do enter our minds, we can deal with them indirectly, for example, by following some time-tested methods of **centering prayer**. When thoughts, including sense perceptions, feelings, images, a reflection, a memory, or whatever, start to hound us, we return gently yet firmly to our sacred word. As the apostle Paul reminds us, "The Spirit ... comes to the aid of our weakness; for we do not know how to pray as we ought, but the Spirit itself intercedes with inexpressible groanings" (Romans 8:26).

Dominic, Saint

(1170-1221) A native of Castile, Spain, Dominic was a student at the University of Palencia from his fourteenth year. He joined the Canons Regular of the Cathedral of Osma, was ordained a priest, and fully expected to continue his scholarly work in the cloister. Little could he have known then that he would be the founder of the Order of Preachers!

His life changed under the guidance of Divine Providence in 1205, when the bishop of Osma asked Dominic to accompany him on a trip to Denmark in service of the King of Castile, who wanted to arrange a marriage for his son. Thus began Dominic's travels. On the way home the two men stopped in Rome to see Pope Innocent.

The Pope asked them to return to the south of France to assist the **Cistercian** monks in combating the heresy of Catharism or Albigensianism with its gnostic and cultic teachings. This Christian heresy separated in a dualistic or Manichaean fashion the spiritual or contemplative world from the earthly or corrupt world, the former being of God, the latter of the **devil**. Adherents to this false belief system, with its purification rituals, had, in Dominic's opinion, lost touch with the essentials of their Catholic **faith**. Those preaching to them seemed to have lost their inspiration. At any rate, they could not compete with the self-limiting ascetic conduct and enthusiasm of the heretics.

Then and there Dominic, by now accompanied by six other men, and inspired by the work of the first apostles, envisioned a new style of religious life and missionary activity that would evangelize by harmonizing informational understanding of doctrine and dogma with formational attention to people's spiritual needs based on the experience of living and working with them. The Order of Preachers or the Black Friars, as they were popularly known, would be trained in theology, become skillful communicators, and travel on foot and without money. Within a year the new order was approved by Rome and the Dominicans began to preach in different parts of Europe, working for the **conversion** of heretics and sinners and calling for vocations.

Though Saint Dominic left no writings, his life is itself his legacy. As he once told a prelate all too eager to condemn everyone outside the fold: "You cannot defeat the enemies of the faith like that. Arm yourself with prayer, not a sword. Wear humility, not fine clothes!" He died in peace among his brothers, leaving them with the words: "My dear sons, these are my bequests: practice **charity** in common; remain humble; stay poor willingly."

1. cf. Gen 3:1-5; Wis 2:24.

E

Eckhart, Meister

(1260-1329) A native of the province of Thuringia in Germany, Eckhart became a Dominican friar. His bent toward learning prompted his superiors to send him to the University of Paris to study theology. Recognized as a man of exceptional brilliance, he held the prestigious chair once occupied by **Saint Thomas Aquinas,** and earned the title "Meister."

When Eckhart returned to Germany, he became prior of the monastery at Erfurt. Some of his talks were transcribed and circulated as instructions to the faithful, who saw in him an eloquent, honest, and compassionate spiritual master. Around 1320, Eckhart wrote for the bereaved Queen Agnes of Hungary the *Book of Divine Consolation*, which contained his famous treatise "On Detachment." There he defines his principal ideas on the relationship between the human and the divine. In regard to true **detachment**, Eckhart simply believed that "to be empty of all created things is to be full of God, and to be full of created things is to be empty of God."

His popularity as a speaker and a writer opened him to scrutiny by the archbishop of Cologne, who accused him of heresy. Eckhart defended himself to the Holy See, assuring the pope that he might err in thought but never in will and that he was not a heretic. The defense was not accepted. Twenty-eight propositions in his writings were condemned as part of his ecclesiastical trial in 1326. The strain of these accusations of heresy probably placed his mystic sensibility under such duress that he died three years later, saved from having to suffer from the wrongful pronouncement of posthumous excommunication by Pope John XII, a ban that has since been lifted by the Church.

History has shown that Eckhart used paradoxical and quite original formulations to try to grasp the unity of the divine and the human while never obfuscating the immeasurable difference between the "allness" of the Creator and the "nothingness" of us creatures. He preached that good works can only proceed from a good spirit. This kind of other-centered goodness calls for self-emptying and detachment, indeed for the pursuit of God beyond "gods" or those illusory attachments that impede progress to **union** and the final birth of the Word in the soul.

Elizabeth of the Trinity, Saint (1880-1906) Marie Elizabeth Catez was born to a distinguished family in Bourges, France, known for its dedication to both civic and religious concerns. An officer in the French army, her father died when Elizabeth was seven years old, leaving her mother to raise Elizabeth and her sister Marguerite. The three of them moved to Dijon, where Elizabeth blossomed under the firm guidance of her mother into a vivacious and unusually self-possessed child.

At the time of her First Communion on April 19, 1891, perhaps having an inkling to her future vocation to the religious life, she made a vow of virginity. A gifted pianist, a member of the parish choir, and a catechist, this future saint had many friends and admirers, but nothing could displace her attraction to interior prayer. Following a visit to the Carmel in Dijon, where she learned that her name meant "house of God," she knew she had found her true calling.

Like **Saint Thérèse of Lisieux**, whose autobiography she read, Elizabeth would not rest until she entered the cloister. However, her mother made her delay her entrance to the convent until she was twenty-one and had finished her education. As a postulant she began to experience not only a lifelong love for **silence** but also interior trials, similar to the dark nights of sense and spirit described by her spiritual father, **Saint John of the Cross**, and her mother in Carmel, **Saint Teresa of Avila**, whose book *The Way of Perfection* had a profound influence on her.

Elizabeth also loved the Scriptures, especially the Epistles of Saint Paul. There she found the assurance that she had been chosen by Christ before the foundation of the world. By the time of her religious profession in 1903, she experienced a deep **peace** of soul, for she had found Christ everywhere and every activity immersed her more in God. A year later she composed her famous prayer to the **Blessed Trinity**, which is a synthesis of her experience and her spiritual doctrine. It ends with the unforgettable words: "O my Three, my All, my Beatitude, infinite Solitude, Immensity in which I lose myself, I surrender myself to You as Your prey. Bury Yourself in me that I may bury myself in You until I depart to contemplate in Your light the abyss of Your greatness."

Depart Elizabeth soon would, for by 1905, she had begun to experience the symptoms of the illness (Addison's Disease) that would end her life. For the next several months, she could do nothing but abandon herself totally to the Divine Will. After a brief remission of her pain, she suffered yet another relapse, but on May 24, 1906, a few months before her death in November of that year, she reported having received the grace of feeling the presence of God. "It seems to me," she wrote shortly before her death, "that in heaven my mission will be to attract souls by helping them to go out of themselves, in order to cling to God with a very simple and loving movement, and to keep them in that great interior silence which allows God to imprint himself on them and to transform them into himself."

When Elizabeth was beatified on November 25, 1984, by Pope John Paul II, he confirmed her legacy to the Church by giving her as a guide to men and women who seek to simplify their lives in **charity** and to make of them an experience of unceasing prayer.

> ## *Encompassed by God*
>
> Having reposed all my hope in the infinite merits of our Lord and Savior Jesus Christ, being encompassed with this protection, I enjoyed a greater satisfaction in the midst of this raging tempest, than when I was wholly delivered from the danger. In very truth, being as I am, the worst of all men, I am ashamed to have shed so many tears of joy, through an excess of heavenly pleasure, when I was just upon the point of perishing ... I humbly prayed [to] our Lord that he would not free me from the danger of my shipwreck, unless it were to reserve me for greater dangers, to his own glory, and for his service. God has often shown me by an inward discovery, from how many perils and sufferings he has delivered me by the prayers and sacrifices of those of the society.
>
> *–Saint Francis Xavier*

Eucharist

As we read in the *Catechism*, **faith**, **hope**, and love find their "all in all" in the Eucharist [1326]. Indeed this is *"bread of angels, bread from heaven, medicine of immortality,* [1331].[1] Our Mass (*Missa*) is called "Holy," for at its center the mystery of salvation is accomplished; we are then sent forth (*missio*) to fulfill God's will in fidelity to the life form (our call) and the lifestyle (our situation) to which God has beckoned us from the beginning.

What makes the Eucharist so central a sacrament is its institution by Christ himself when he knew that his hour to leave us had come [1337]. It was Christ who said to those at table, "This is my body which is given for you. Do this in remembrance of me.... This cup which is poured out for you is the New

Covenant in my blood" (Luke 22:7-20) [quoted in 1339]. As Jesus passes over to the Father, he leaves us with the extraordinary gift of the new Passover, celebrated in the Eucharist [1338-1340]. He asks us to do what we do in memory of him until he comes again in glory [1341].

So essential is this celebration that we could not live as Christians without it—not only on Sunday but daily, at least in intention. As the Eucharist is "the center of the Church's life," so must it be the center of our spiritual life [1343]. When we gather for the liturgy of the Word, the readings, homily, and general intercessions, when we proceed to celebrate the liturgy of the Eucharist with the priest presiding, we experience together "one single act of worship" [1346].[2] All parts of our celebration coalesce as one graced and gracious movement. All in attendance, from the people in the pew to the Eucharistic ministers, have an important role to play [1348], culminating in the offerings by the priest of bread and wine that will become at the moment of consecration Christ's Body and Blood.

Every time we celebrate the Eucharist, we await the coming of the Lord in glory. Every time we approach the altar, we thank God for this privilege to break "the one bread that provides the medicine of immortality, the antidote for death, and the food that makes us live forever in Jesus Christ" [1405].[3]

Eudes, Saint John

(1601-80) Feeling from the time of his youth in Normandy, France, the call to be a priest, Eudes met Pierre Cardinal de Bérulle (1575-1629) under whose influence he joined the Paris Oratory, where he received ordination in 1625. Characteristic of his priesthood was his **devotion** to the sick and dying. His care for the poor knew no bounds during two outbreaks of the plague. Later he preached missions, earned a deserved reputation as a confessor, and helped many people to liberate their hearts and minds from a harsh Jansenistic view of life and God.

In 1641 Eudes founded a refuge for women, staffed by the Visitandine Sisters. He soon saw that these sisters might form the core of a new order. It became, under his inspiration, the Sisters of Our Lady of Charity of the Refuge. A few years later, he received a special call from God to pursue clerical reform. Saint John left the Oratorians to found the Congregation of Jesus and Mary, whose central mission was to deepen the spiritual and intellectual formation of the clergy, symbolized by their union with the Sacred Heart of Jesus and the Immaculate Heart of Mary. He was accorded recognition as the Father, Doctor, and Apostle of these devotions following his canonization in 1925 by Pope Pius XI.

Evagrius Ponticus

(c. 345-400) A contemporary of the three Cappadocian Fathers and saints **Basil the Great**, **Gregory Nazianus**, by whom he was ordained a deacon, and **Gregory of Nyssa**, Evagrius was an eloquent speaker, a brilliant teacher, and an austere hermit. His own influence and reputation came to rival that of his mentors. His counsels on spiritual living (*The Praktikos* and *Chapters on Prayer*) are storehouses of wisdom, relevant for every age.

Evagrius saw his monastic life, which he lived in Egypt from 383 onward, as a blessed though bloodless martyrdom. He had the privilege of coming into contact not only with Hellenic intellectualism in the writings of **Origen** but also with the practical counsels of the first generation of the **Desert Fathers**, notably Saint Macarius the Great. From this rich treasury of wisdom and discipline he learned the lesson that **mysticism** has to be grounded in **asceticism** just as **contemplation** has to bear fruit in **charity**.

Evagrius' gifts of psychological insight and vivid description enabled him to analyze and define the various stages of the spiritual way. Writers in the East like **Saint John Climacus** are indebted to his description of the soul's journey to God. According to Evagrius, the ascetic way of keeping the commandments (*praktike*) aims to purify the unruly passions of the soul and thereby to remove obstacles to contemplation. Such discipline guides the soul into a state of *apatheia*, tranquility or deep calm. This state gives rise in turn to *agape* or the love that draws us into the heart of God.

The mystical way, as Evagrius understands it, proceeds by degrees from natural contemplation (*theoria*), using the senses and reason to progressive contemplation (*theologia*), in which the intellect rises beyond forms and figures to behold in pure **faith** and heavenly luminosity the living God. The main barriers to this ascent are the **capital sins**. Evagrius is the first to identify as the fiercest demon of them all, the noonday **devil**, who preys on the monk's peace of mind. To defeat him is to gain victory over the other vices.

Examination of Conscience

By this act we seriously contemplate the state of our soul ("Am I living my life in conformity to the will of God?") and the nature of our sin ("How and to what degree have I deviated from God's commands and the teachings of the Church?"). Such an honest, inner look at our lives can be done anytime, ideally daily in the morning, at noon, or in the evening, but it is especially necessary to examine our conscience prior to receiving the sacrament of Penance and Reconciliation.

Avoiding scrupulosity and a fixation on "how many times" we did or did not do this or that is important. Rather, by focusing on the **mercy** and **forgiveness** of God, we strive since our last confession to remember particular words, actions, or omissions of ours, which may be sinful. More importantly, we try to focus on the motives, dispositions, and attitudes that led to these sins in the first place. It is wise to examine our relationships to God and others in light of the Commandments and the **Beatitudes**. When we listen to what our conscience tells us, we can hear God, the Supreme Good, speaking to our heart.

A well-formed and informed conscience is a wonderful companion on the journey to God. The education of conscience begins when we are young, but it never stops. The benefits of regular self-examination, resting on the Word of God and on the teachings of the Church, and made in the presence of a loving God, are many. This practice helps us to become upright, moral citizens, humble women and men who live by the truth and love it. An honest examination of conscience increases our capacity to make prudent judgments, especially about ourselves, and to pray for guidance, indeed to seek it, also in the confessional, when moral dilemmas face us. Above all, this spiritual discipline results in our willingness to assume responsibility for our acts and not to try to hide anything from God, "for God is greater than our hearts and knows everything" (1 John 3:20).

1. St. Ignatius of Antioch, *Ad Eph.* 20, 2:SCh 10, 76.
2. SC 56.
3. Lg 3; St. Ignatius of Antioch, *Ad Eph.* 20, 2:SCh 10, 76.

F

Faith

With the all-seeing eyes of faith, we can behold the hand of God in whatever circumstances he places us. Faith allows us to transform ugliness into beauty, malice into kindness, the night of doubt itself into a glad experience of grace. As we read in the *Catechism,* we make our first "profession of faith" when we are baptized "in the name of the Father and of the Son and of the Holy Spirit" [189].[1] We continue to profess what we believe every time we recite the Apostles' or the Nicene Creed, make the sign of the cross, pray the mysteries of the rosary, read the lives of the saints, and venerate the martyrs.

The *Catechism* defines faith as "the theological virtue by which we believe in God and believe all that he has said and revealed to us, and that the Holy Church proposes for our belief ..." [1814]. As believers, we come to know and do the will of God as a consequence of accepting Jesus Christ, the only begotten Son of God, as our Savior. Faith is a gift we neither merit nor deserve; however, once received, it challenges us to commit ourselves to the gospel demands of love and service.

The witness of faith is a blessing worthy of any price. As we read in the Gospel of Matthew (10:32-33): "Everyone who acknowledges me before others I will acknowledge before my heavenly Father. But whoever denies me before others, I will deny before my heavenly Father." According to **Saint John of the Cross**, faith is the only proximate means to union with God, and, by extension, to the performance of all the good works that flow from it.

For Our Sake

Even if all masters were dead and all books were burned, we should still find instruction enough in his holy life, for he himself, and no other, is the way. Let us follow [Jesus] with all our strength, and we too shall reach the precious goal to which he has gone before us, for our sake.

–*John Tauler*

Faustina, Saint Maria

See **Kowalska, Saint Maria Faustina**

Forgiveness

Giving and receiving forgiveness is a central discipline of the Christian spiritual life. Jesus sees a direct link between our forgiveness of others and God's forgiveness of us: "If you forgive others their transgressions, your heavenly Father will forgive you. But if you do not forgive others, neither will your Father forgive your transgressions" (Matthew 6:14-15). Though forgiveness of sin is an act of God toward the sinner, Jesus Christ, by virtue of his divinity, assumed this prerogative and passed it on to his Church as a divinely commissioned task. As the apostle Peter said to the first converts under his care, "Repent and be baptized, everyone of you, in the name of Jesus Christ for the forgiveness of your sins; and you will receive the gift of the holy Spirit" (Acts 2:38).

The sacrament of Penance and Reconciliation is also called in the Catholic Church the *"sacrament of forgiveness."* As the *Catechism* says, it is "by the priest's sacramental absolution [that] God grants the penitent 'pardon and peace'" [1424].[2] The worthy reception of this sacrament requires three things: contrition or sorrow for the sins we have committed; confession or telling of all our sins to a priest with **humility** and complete sincerity for the purpose of obtaining forgiveness; and penance to help us improve our relationships with God and others.

A beautiful parable of restored relationships and of God's love for the repentant sinner is that of the Prodigal Son in Luke 15:11-32. We learn from this story that to forgive means to give to another in the name of the Lord something of the love he has given to us. Is it any wonder that we pray daily in the **Lord's Prayer** to be forgiven of our sins as we forgive those who trespass against us?

Francis de Sales, Saint

(1567-1622) With the **obedience** characteristic of his nature, Francis followed his family's wishes that he study law rather than enter the seminary, as he wanted to do. Not long after he attained his law degree, he turned his back on what would have been a brilliant career to pursue a priestly life.

After his ordination in 1593, he was sent to minister to Catholics in the region of Lake Geneva. Due to de Sales' compassionate nature and his knowledge of both civil and canon law, in 1599 Pope Clement VIII appointed him coadjutor to the bishop of Geneva, a position requiring great grace and diplomatic skills since the area around the lake was predominantly Calvinist. His bent toward reconciliation versus revenge was rewarded, for three years later he himself became the bishop of that region.

It was in Geneva that Francis not only foiled several assassination attempts but also began to be recognized as a brilliant preacher and a man endowed with exceptional spiritual gifts. In fact, a Calvinist minister in Geneva said of him, "If we honored any man as a saint, I know no one since the days of the apostles more worthy of it than this man." His gentle heart and sense of self-sacrifice endeared him to the people. Many were reconciled to the Church thanks to him. In controversy, he was a model of good manners, sensitive to others, moderate in judgment, clear in expression, dignified and modest. The depth at which Francis heard the **call to holiness** is evidenced in his two most famous books, both spiritual classics, *Treatise on the Love of God* (1607) and *Introduction to the Devout Life* (1608).

In 1604 de Sales agreed to be the mentor and spiritual guide of Jane Frances de Chantel, the saintly widow and spiritual friend with whom he would exchange many letters of direction and found a new religious order for women, the nuns of the Order of the Visitation. As a superb spiritual director and one of the leading figures of the Catholic Reformation, Francis also appealed to ordinary people in all walks of life to develop their spirituality not apart from but in the midst of their social, familial, and professional circumstances. His methods of direction were gentle yet firm, stressing moderation, not excessive forms of piety. He believed in the basic goodness of the human soul and its innate hunger for God. He not only introduced his readers to the devout life as a way to find God wherever one was; he also taught workable methods of **meditation** based on the instinct of love and fidelity to everyday occasions of grace. A famous saying of this Doctor of the Church and patron saint of Catholic journalists is: "The measure of love is to love without measure."

Francis of Assisi, Saint

(1182-1226) A native of the town of Assisi in Italy, Francis was the son of a wealthy merchant family. As a youth he led a frivolous, carefree life typical of a young gentleman of his social standing, but all that changed in the year 1206. Then an experience of sickness amidst the devastation of civil war sobered and steadied him.

One day in the Church of San Damiano he seemed to hear Christ saying from the cross, "Francis, repair my falling house." Taking these words literally, he sold some goods from his father's warehouse to pay for the repair work. Before long he was so intent on fulfilling a divine call that his earthly father disinherited and disowned him.

Instead of despairing, the penniless Francis wed "Lady Poverty" and began to live on alms while continuing to repair churches. In 1209 Francis realized that his real mission was to build up the Church by preaching repentance, living a life of **poverty**, **chastity**, and **obedience**, and conforming his entire being to Christ. A few years later, Pope Innocent III authorized him and eleven companions to be roving preachers of the gospel of Jesus Christ and to live in complete simplicity. Thus began the Friars Minor. Shortly thereafter, he founded with **Saint Clare of Assisi** the first community of Poor Clares.

Before his death Francis produced a revised version of his rule. In it he reiterated his insistence on evangelical poverty as the only path to true freedom. Two years before his death, Francis received the gift of the stigmata, the graced phenomenon of having on his own body marks resembling the wounds of the Crucified Savior. The pain Francis experienced was nothing compared to the joy he received. Having perhaps outdone himself in the realm of mortification, he offered an apology to his body, "Brother Ass," before he welcomed "Sister Death."

Saint Francis is universally admired as a man of tremendous spiritual insight and power, whose consuming love for Jesus Christ and redeemed creation found expression in all that he said and did. His visionary leadership continues to inspire people of his own and other faiths to live in a spirit of simplicity and service, to delight in creation, and to embrace the cross with "a correct **faith**, a certain **hope**, a perfect **charity**." So recognizable was Francis' holiness that a mere two years after his death he was canonized a saint.

Franciscan Spirituality

The spirituality of **Saint Francis of Assisi** permeates the teachings of his order and the writings of his followers, notably **Saint Clare of Assisi** and **Saint Bonaventure**. The Franciscan way is "Christocentric." Francis, himself a Christ-figure, lived in the flesh the mystery of incarnation, adoption, redemption, and restoration. He saw the entire cosmos as a revelation of the eternal designs of our loving Creator. So profound is Francis' love of creation that it overflows in frequent prayers of praise and thanksgiving. His canticles summarize his **abandonment to Divine Providence** and his conviction that Jesus not only draws repentant sinners to a new order of relationship but turns the entire universe into one continuous hymn of praise.

The hallmarks of Franciscan spirituality are: (1) We are called to contemplate with awe and wonder the marvelous unity that weaves its way through the works of God. (2) Every facet of life reflects this unity. (3) Diverse and detailed as our unique lives may be, they find their common ground in God's love for us and our love for God and in our communion with one another. (4) The principal of universal love is the force ruling and directing all things. (5) Our human efforts originate in grace and are supported by grace. (6) Christ is both the object of our contemplation and the means by which we come to know the Persons of the **Blessed Trinity**.

Some essential exercises of Franciscan spirituality include, besides **unceasing prayer** and praise, reliance on the **Eucharist**, which vivifies and activates our soul and makes possible our transformation in Christ; love for the **Blessed Virgin Mary** and for every cell in Christ's Mystical Body, especially the poor and the outcast; participation in the liturgical life of the Church; and adherence to various ascetic practices, not as ends in themselves but as openings to God, who, in Francis' words, lives and rules "in perfect Trinity and simple Unity."

French School of Spirituality

The specific typology of the French School reveals its place in the Catholic mainstream and discloses its characteristic attitudes and applications. The masters of this school are, among others, Pierre Cardinal de Bérulle, Jean-Jacques Olier, **Saint John Eudes**, and Mother Madeleine de Saint-Joseph. The basic assumption of the French School is that because we are created by God and formed in his image, our lives on earth ought to be pathways and pointers to what we shall be eternally in heaven.

Adherents of this way stress the necessity of basing the spiritual life on the cornerstones of the **faith**; interiorizing the liturgical life; developing a personal union with God; seeing the apostolate as the fruit of **contemplation**; stressing the centrality of the priesthood and the **Eucharist**, the urgent need for evangelization, the role of the **Blessed Virgin Mary** in forming the soul in the image of Christ, and the commission of the laity to cooperate with Christ in the world.

The first emphasis of our journey to the hearts of Jesus and Mary is *adoration*, a habitual state of soul that consists in acknowledging always and everywhere the greatness and goodness of the Trinity. This state of adoring love, proceeding from the core of one's being, calls for an attitude of *abasement* before the supreme majesty, for a posture of deep **humility.**

To live in this state of adoring and self-emptying love, Christians must imitate in their everyday spiritual life three facets of Jesus' own love for the Father. We must *adhere* first of all to his attributes and virtues and strive to reproduce them in our own state of life by rejecting sin and remaining open to grace. Like Jesus, we Christians also must try to *annihilate* all traces of self-interest and act only and always to glorify God. We must, in Olier's words, "live entirely for God in Christ Jesus," becoming "annihilated" in regard to our own plans and committing ourselves as disciples to the Son, who, through the Holy Spirit, is in us to enable us to live wholly with the Father. As Jesus accepted the Father's will in everything, so must we say with increasing fidelity, "Not my will but thine be done."

The most vivid exemplar of this profound surrender is the **Blessed Virgin Mary**. She models in a magnificent way the third facet, *abnegation*. Jesus will live in us, as he dwelt in Mary's womb and in her heart, only to the degree that we joyfully "disappropriate" ourselves, that is, renounce proprietorship over ourselves and become God's servants.

Strengthened by grace and responsive to the call of the Spirit, we can then accept and worthily fulfill our *apostolic* duty to teach all nations and to build up the body of Christ in his holy Church. Once we allow our frail, human hearts to become more and more like the adoring, adhering, annihilated, abnegated hearts of Jesus and Mary, we can carry out the work we are called to do "on earth as it is in heaven."

Fruits of the Holy Spirit

This is the designation the Church gives collectively to the acts that result from the Spirit's working in the Christian heart, mind, and will to bring to fruition the graces we receive at **Baptism**. When we respond to these graces and inspirations our lives bear good fruit and become "godly."

In his counsels to the Galatians on how to live in conformity to Christ, Saint Paul contrasts the bad fruits of evil living (contention, murder, idolatry, hatred, rivalry, furious outbursts, selfish acts, and jealousy) to the good fruits of the people of God led by the Spirit. They are, by contrast, "love, joy, peace, patience, kindness, generosity, faithfulness, gentleness, self-control" (Galatians 5:22-23). To these nine the Church adds modesty, goodness, and **chastity**, bringing these fruits to a total of twelve.

The apostle gives us a simple rule to obey if we want, as a familiar expression suggests, to bloom where we are planted. He says, "If we live in the Spirit, let us also follow the Spirit" (Galatians 5:25). The more we renounce ourselves, the more we walk in and by the Spirit of the living God.

As the *Catechism* reminds us, wherever we witness these fruits in action, we see the "perfections that the Holy Spirit forms in us" [1832].

1. Mt 28:19.
2. *OP* 46: formula of absolution.

Gerson, John

(1363-1429) Educator, theologian, preacher, and chancellor of the University of Paris from 1395 until his death, Gerson played a significant role in helping to resolve the Great Schism in the Western Church revolving around the papacy in Rome and a rival papacy in Avignon. He also sought in the midst of this tumultuous age to bring the ways of **contemplative prayer** to groups of people not in academic or ecclesiastical life, starting with the members of his own family.

Respected equally by his colleagues and the common folk, Gerson became one of the most known and quoted experts on the spiritual life in medieval Europe. His monumental work, *The Mountain of Contemplation*, reveals his indebtedness to **Saint Bernard of Clairvaux** and **Saint Gregory the Great**. In these two favorite authors, he saw the same synthesis he sought between mind and heart, intellect and emotion. Other major influences on his sixty-six works on the spiritual life include **Saint Augustine, Saint Bonaventure, Richard of Saint Victor**, and **Pseudo-Dionysius**.

Gerson concluded from his reading and study that mystical theology does not require the dissolution of rational structures of the mind; rather it elevates the mind from mere learning to wisdom. It goes beyond an intellectual grasp of truths to an encounter with the Truth, uniting the soul to God in an ecstasy of love.

Gertrude the Great, Saint

(1256-1301) Saint Gertrude entered the Benedictine Abbey of Helfta in Saxony in 1260, at the tender age of four or five. Although she followed the monastic rule outwardly, by her own admission she focused primarily on secular studies. All that changed in her twenty-sixth year, when the Lord appeared to her in the form of a beautiful young man and invited her to a complete **conversion** of life, characterized by intimate union with him.

From that moment on, Gertrude devoted her entire existence to God and the care of neighbor for his sake. She struck a balance between study and service, **worship** and work. In true **Benedictine** fashion, she subordinated her love of learning to her desire for God.

Gertrude was granted extraordinary mystical favors, one of the most notable being an intense awareness of

God's loving presence in her soul. Her **humility** and consequent reticence made her long for **solitude,** but her common sense assured her that she had been granted these graces for the good of others. She determined that God required her to be a herald of divine love, symbolized in her life and writings by her **devotion** to the saving and transforming power of the Sacred Heart of Jesus.

> *God's Will*
>
> I had continuously to learn to accept God's will—not as I wished it to be, not as it might have been, but as it actually was at the moment. And it was through the struggle to do this that spiritual growth and a greater appreciation of his will took place.
>
> –*Father Walter Ciszek*

Gifts of the Holy Spirit

The first and most essential gift of the Spirit to us is love. This gift contains the seven dispositions or virtues that make us open to receive and follow with docility the promptings of the Holy Spirit, these being wisdom, understanding, counsel, fortitude, knowledge, piety, and fear of the Lord. We see each of these gifts lived in their fullness by our Lord, Jesus Christ.

In addition to these seven gifts, the Spirit also dispenses at God's bidding certain special graces, called **charisms,** by which, according to the *Catechism,* he makes the servants of God fit and ready to understand the tasks and offices they hold for the sake of reviewing and building up the Church [1898]. In receiving these gifts, as we do in a special way through the sacrament of **Confirmation,** we are called not only to practice other virtues more perfectly but also to open our human spirit to receive the inspirations of the Holy Spirit.

The gift of adoption, like all the other gifts of the Holy Spirit, must never be taken for granted. As Saint Paul proclaims in the Letter to the Romans: "For those who are led by the Spirit of God are children of God. For you did not receive a spirit of slavery to fall back into fear, but you received a spirit of adoption, through which we cry, *Abba,* 'Father!' The Spirit itself bears witness with our spirit that we are children of God, and if children, then heirs, heirs of God and joint heirs with Christ...." (Romans 8:14-17). If we live our lives keeping this truth in mind, we can expect that we shall have to pay a price—the price of living the cross, for only if we suffer with Christ may we also be "glorified with him" (Romans 8:17).

Gregory the Great, Saint

(540-604) Born in Rome at a time in the history of the Western Church when the Empire was like a great crumbling mountain, Gregory wrote in 593: "Ruins upon ruins everywhere! Where is the senate? Where are the people? ... We, the few who are left, are menaced every day by the sword and innumerable trials ... Deserted Rome is in flames."

Twenty years earlier, at the age of thirty-five, he had interrupted a brilliant public career and, under the impetus of God's call, resigned his secular honors. He turned his palatial residence into a Benedictine monastery called Saint Andrew's. He thereafter established six additional monasteries on the family property. Thanks to his highly developed liturgical sense, he initiated reforms in ritual and music, notably "Gregorian Chant," which still inspire the Church today.

Diplomatically gifted as he was, Gregory served as Papal Nuncio to Constantinople until 584. After sincere efforts to evade his election, he became pope in 590, determined to be a leader whose first commitment was to be the "servant of God's servants," a title still in use today. God raised up in Gregory a pope whose goodness and brilliance enabled him to carry on his shoulders not only the weight of what was best in Roman culture but also what Christian theology needed to achieve if it was to address the spiritual and material welfare of the people.

In trying to uphold the administrative, social, ecclesial, and moral claims of an ideal Christian society, Gregory shows that both the *vita contemplativa* and the *vita activa* are valid ways of discipleship. Addressing God in characteristic **humility**, he prayed, "But in the shipwreck of this life, sustain me, I beseech you, with the plank of your prayers, so that, as my weight is sinking me down, you may uplift me with your meritorious hand."

Gregory Nazianzus, Saint

(c. 329-90) By nature a shy, quiet, and contemplative man, Gregory was called from the solitary life to the front lines in the fight for orthodoxy, defending the Church against **Arianism.** Gregory joined the monastery of his friend **Saint Basil the Great**, and the two of them worked to perfect the new monastic principles that would influence community life in the East and in the West.

Ordained against his will, Gregory began his life's work by sharpening his understanding of the **Blessed Trinity**. He did so with such depth and understanding that the Church named him "The Theologian." As Gregory's fame spread, his enemies multiplied, especially among the Arians, who continued to persecute him to the point of physical violence. In 379, the year of Basil's death, Gregory arrived in Constantinople and turned his place of lodging into the Church of the Resurrection, where he preached his famous sermons on the Trinity. He defined for the first time the characteristics of the Three Persons as the Father's "unbegottenness," the Son's "begottenness," and the "procession" of the Holy Spirit, while showing what they have in common: that they are—all Three—uncreated and divine.

The legacy he left is as vital today as it was in his time. According to Gregory, to live the divine life or to seek "divinization" means that one "should fulfill the commandments as perfectly as possible by ministering to the poor, exercising hospitality, tending the sick, persevering in psalmody, prayer, groaning, tears, prostration on the ground, restraints upon the belly, mortification of the senses, of impulse, of laughter, control of the tongue, lulling the flesh by the power of the spirit.... These ways one must tread, not that way only which depends on eloquence."

After only a few months as bishop of Constantinople, where he had done much to build up the local church, Gregory decided to return to Nazianzus. In 383, he left public life for good and spent his final years writing religious poetry in the solitude of his garden and composing his *De Vita Sua*.

Gregory of Nyssa, Saint

(c. 335-c. 395) Holiness surrounded Saint Gregory. In his immediate family alone, his paternal grandmother, both of his parents, and Gregory himself were declared "saints." His elder brother and teacher, **Saint Basil the Great**, instilled in Gregory a love for the Scriptures and the works of Greek fathers like **Origen** and **Saint Clement of Alexandria**. His brother Basil and their mutual friend, **Saint Gregory Nazianzus**, persuaded Gregory to become a priest after he had married and earned his living for some years as a man of letters.

Basil, who was then archbishop of Caesarea, named Gregory bishop of the town of Nyssa in his district so that he might be of help to him in the struggle against **Arianism.** By 379, he was acknowledged to be one of the leading theologians of the Christian East.

To assure the depth of his own spiritual life, Gregory detached himself from wealth and family connections to seek a life of **asceticism** in **solitude**. Prayer and fasting made him an early proponent of the apophatic way or the way of unknowing, as exemplified in his book on *The Life of Moses*. This masterpiece offers readers a spiritual sense of the Scriptures and reveals how reading the Bible can elevate the soul to God.

Gregory saw the life of the spirit as a growth process, a continual straining ahead for what is to come. The spiritual ascent takes place in three stages, symbolized by the Lord's revelations of himself to Moses, first in light, then in the cloud, and, finally, in the dark. This **mysticism** of knowing God beyond all intellectual knowledge about God, of experiencing God's presence in the dark cloud of incomprehensibility, was a new theme in Christianity that would pass into the Western Church through the works of **Pseudo-Dionysius, Meister Eckart,** ***The Cloud of Unknowing***, and **Saint John of the Cross**. All would concur with Gregory's conviction that "human speech finds it impossible to express that reality which transcends all thought and every concept."

As one of the great Cappadocian Fathers of the fourth century, Saint Gregory influenced the formulation of the Church's Trinitarian doctrine and is best known for the range and richness of his ascetic and mystical theology. He describes the spiritual life as an ascent from darkness to light to deeper darkness. The true enjoyment of the soul consists in never ceasing to ascend toward the "kindred Deity," who draws that which is his own to himself.

Guardian Angels

Angels are spiritual, noncorporeal, celestial beings, the messengers of God and our guardians. At the center of the angelic world is the Son of God, the Christ, who commands the angels and receives for eternity their songs of praise. No angel can ever reach the stature of Christ. Was it not out of envy that Lucifer, angel of light, became Satan, prince of darkness, whose seduction of humans preceded the Fall?

Even as children we are warned of the influence of the "bad angels," the **devils**, who prowl around seeking whom they may devour, and who are opposed by the good angels, especially the guardian angel personally assigned to each of us. The angels who serve God continue to serve us as well. Though they grasp the truth wholly and know it by simple understanding, they do not interfere with our freedom of choice.

When Adam and Eve sinned and were banished by an angel of God from the Garden of Eden, it would require nothing less than the Incarnation and Redemption to expiate our nature from evil's hellish bonds. In Jesus Christ, God did not assume an angelic nature but a human one, becoming like us in all things but sin. Angels, who are and remain immaterial, have a significant role to play in our lives by guarding them as the precious gifts they are and by guiding us to truths that bring us closer to God.

Though angels have powers far beyond our own, they share in the beatitude that is ours through the death and resurrection of Jesus. They bring his Word to us in special ways, as in visions and revelations when the angel Gabriel announced to the **Blessed Virgin Mary** that she had found favor with God and would bear his Son (Luke 1: 26-38). Later it was an angel who informed Joseph that he had to protect his family by withdrawing to Egypt and an angel who told him when to return to Judea (Matthew 2:13-15; 19-22). Still later Jesus received his Father's commands from the angels; it was also their duty to comfort him (Matthew 4:11; Luke 22:43).

Guigo II

(d. 1188) Little is known of this **Carthusian** monk save that he was the ninth prior of the motherhouse, the Grand Chartreuse, until his resignation from this post in 1180. After that he spent the remainder of his life in **solitude**, acquiring among his brothers a singular reputation for sanctity. Attributed to him are three influential works: *The Ladder of Monks*, with its goal of contemplative union; *Twelve Meditations;* and a reflection on the *Magnificat*. In many ways these texts mirror the entire thrust of the Western monastic and mystical tradition from **Saint Augustine** to **Saint Benedict** while influencing the last pre-Reformation renewal movement, the ***Devotio Moderna.***

The analogy of the "ladder" or the "stairway" for depicting the soul's interior ascent to God is an ancient one, starting with Jacob's vision in the Book of Genesis. In the third century **Origen** used the analogy to present the sequence of the threefold path developed by later authors like **Pseudo-Dionysius, John Climacus, Walter Hilton**, and **Saint John of the Cross.**

According to this analogy, one's progress in **contemplation** proceeds upward through three ascending grades: **purgation** for beginners, **illumination** for proficients, and **union** for the perfect. Guigo's original contribution was to present the image of the spiritual life as rungs on a ladder one must climb step by step, starting with the reading of Holy Scripture.

To climb this ladder is to reorder the natural affections of the heart into a loving desire for God and a mystical sense of oneness with his Word. Guigo called love the "cross of the spirit" that fastens us to Christ and readies us for the sight of God, whom we long to see face-to-face in the Beatific Vision. "Reading seeks for the sweetness of a blessed life, meditation perceives it, prayer asks for it, contemplation tastes it." He further summarizes this fourfold movement of formation as follows:

> Reading is the careful study of the scriptures, concentrating all one's powers on it. Meditation is the busy application of the mind to seek with the help of one's own reason for knowledge of hidden truth. Prayer is the heart's devoted turning to God to drive away evil and obtain what is good. Contemplation is when the mind is in some sort lifted up to God and held above itself, so that it tastes the joys of everlasting sweetness.

Hadewijch

(d. 1282) A Flemish Beguine of the thirteenth century, Hadewijch draws upon the power of poetry commingled with heartfelt prayer to communicate her spiritual message. Like **Saint Teresa of Avila** in the sixteenth century, this visionary from Antwerp was graced with the dual gifts of mystical union and literary genius. As a member of the most notable women's movement of her day, she dedicated herself to a life of Christian spirituality in the "cloister of the world."

Hadewijch understood that God had called her to communicate to other seekers the profound knowledge of mystical theology he granted to her. She directed her words of wisdom and her works of **charity** to the younger members of her community, for whom she felt a special affection. In her time she knew little fame. She led and preferred the hidden life of Jesus of Nazareth. As a result, her ecstatic writings went largely unknown until the nineteenth century.

Hadewijch's poetic paradoxical style enabled her to portray at once the humanity and divinity of Christ and the Trinity and unity of God. She believed that the empowerment of human love by divine love enables us to offer ourselves in self-giving love to others. "Therefore," she writes, "works with faith must precede love; then love will set them on fire."

Hildegard of Bingen, Saint

(1098-1179) Born into a noble German family of ten children, young Hildegard was placed in the care of a holy anchoress, Jutta, who raised her until she was eighteen and old enough to decide for herself to enter a nearby Benedictine abbey. After Jutta's death in 1136, Hildegard herself became the prioress of a new foundation inspired by the holy woman under whose guidance she had grown in wisdom, age, and grace.

Since her earliest youth Hildegard had received visions concerning the Word of God in Scripture and the imprint of this divine Word in nature. She saw these revelations with the eyes of her spirit, heard God's voice with the ears of her heart.

Although Hildegard had confided in Jutta about the nature of these visions, eventually she sought and received ecclesial approbation from the archbishop of Mainz. The text she wrote inspired by her visions was judged to be orthodox, and so she continued to write her *Scivias.* These texts concerned the relationship between God and humanity and the cosmos, including powerful insights into the rupturing of creation by sin and its restoration by the Redeemer.

When Hildegard moved her community to a new site near Bingen, the opposition she encountered from the monks who lived nearby sickened her to the point of death, but she prevailed. Subsequently, she made preaching tours throughout the Rhineland, shared her spiritual thoughts with a wide list of correspondents, including kings and popes, composed original religious music, and risked to divulge her unusual knowledge of medicine and physiology. Hildegard's sensitivity for the ecology of the earth and her commitment to the goodness of creation strike a contemporary note, as does the holistic vision she had of a life lived in harmony with God.

Hilton, Walter

(c. 1343-96) An Augustinian canon from the priory of Thurgarton in Yorkshire, Hilton is one of the outstanding English mystics of the fourteenth century. He is best known for his work *The Scale of Perfection,* which follows the style of mystics and spiritual masters like **Blessed John Ruysbroeck** of the Rhineland School and **John Tauler** of the Dominican School. The imagery of a stairway or a ladder is also mindful of the writings of **John Climacus**.

The first book of Hilton's *Scale,* addressed to an anchoress, teaches the means by which a soul made in God's image (*Imago Dei*) may advance toward perfection by reforming that which has been deformed by sin. Following the lead of grace, one may be transformed into "another Christ" (*Alter Christus*) in whom the likeness to God has been restored. Hilton articulates this resurrected relationship as an exchange of love letters between the soul and Jesus, which results in his driving out of one's heart "depression and weariness, doubts and fears." The Lord makes "glad and merry in him those who trust and believe in all his promises, meekly awaiting the fulfillment of his will."

In the second book, Hilton distinguishes between the active or ascetic life and the contemplative or mystical life. Here we find a description of what it means to take up one's cross and follow Christ, based, it would seem, on his own experience as a hermit. He explains in a wise yet balanced and eminently practical way, appealing to readers across the ages, that **conversion** does not mean merely turning from sin to virtue; it is a movement that draws one from an outwardly professed Christianity to complete union with

> ### *Holy Spirit of God*
>
> As for fasts and vigils and prayer, and almsgiving, and every good deed done for Christ's sake, they are only means of acquiring the Holy Spirit of God. To welcome this Guest into our hearts will lead us to ultimate union with God and toward that unity of the human race wherein all shall acquire the peace and joy God promised in his Son.
>
> –*Saint Seraphim of Sarov*

God. For him, knowledge "is the salvation of a man's soul in everlasting life, and the goals of all other kinds of knowledge in themselves are only vanity and passing delight—unless they are converted by grace to this goal of salvation."

Hope

The *Catechism* defines hope as "the theological virtue by which we desire the kingdom of heaven and eternal life as our happiness, placing our trust in Christ's promises and relying not on our own strength, but on the help of the grace of the Holy Spirit" [1817].

To hope is to anticipate the opportunity for formation that resides in every obstacle. Because hope focuses on the unfailing promises of God, it protects us from the self-centeredness that blocks the flow of **charity**. That is why hope stretches us toward heaven and gives us the courage to persevere "to the end" (Matthew 10:22). In the words of G.K. Chesterton, "As long as matters are really hopeful, hope is a mere flattery or platitude; it is only when everything is hopeless that hope begins to be a strength at all. Like all the Christian virtues, it is as unreasonable as it is indispensable."

Hopkins, Gerard Manley

(1844-89) A Jesuit priest and poet, Hopkins is acknowledged to be one of the greatest stylistic innovators in the annals of English poetry. Hopkins spent most of his life fulfilling obscure religious assignments, including the drudgery (to him) of teaching the classics at the Catholic University in Dublin.

Hopkins had a hypersensitive constitution and suffered all his life from poor health. Yet he combines an intense feeling for nature with an aesthetic awareness of its divine origins. He accepted that the only lasting goal of life was to be conformed to the **charity** of Christ, who "plays in ten thousand places/ Lovely in limbs, and lovely in eyes not his/to the Father through the features of men's faces." On June 8, 1889, he died of typhoid fever, but he left a legacy of poetry that celebrates the victory of the "Giver of breath and bread."

Humility

This virtue, along with **detachment** and **charity**, is named by **Saint Teresa of Avila** as an essential step on the way to union with the Triune God. In her book *The Way of Perfection*, she calls humility the one virtue which embraces all the others because it counters the one vice that most separates us from Christ, pride or vainglory. If we are to imitate Christ, we must do so from what **Saint John of the Cross** identifies as the center of our humility.

Both saints agree that real humility leads us to listen to who we most deeply are. It is less a matter of focusing on our misery and more on coming to an awareness of our dependency on God's love and **mercy**.

The saints assure us that great progress in holiness occurs when we resist vain reasonings and defensive postures; take on lowly tasks; avoid the privileges of rank and power; disengage ourselves from excesses of praise or blame; and bear with dishonor, ridicule, and misunderstanding. Only in this way do we model our lives on the humility of Jesus and Mary with real determination, not wavering for reasons of worldly honor but walking, as Saint Teresa says, in the truth of who we are.

I

Ignatian Spirituality

At the core of the Ignatian way is Ignatius' own story, for he was blessed through suffering with a change of heart that made him an intense lover of God and others. *The Spiritual Exercises* of Saint Ignatius record his conversion experience, including his awareness of the need for competent direction in helping one discern, for example, the meaning of **consolation** and **desolation**, good and evil movements of the spirit, and the way to devote one's whole life to the love and service of God. At the heart of the *Exercises* is the process of Ignatian **discernment**, in which one pays prayerful and careful attention to daily life in dialogue with God's revealed Word in Jesus Christ, in the Bible, and in the tradition of the Church.

Discernment in this way of prayer entails a five-step process:

1. Being receptive to the dynamics of God's love active in history;
2. Being present to the providential circumstances of our lives and to our interior reactions and responses;
3. Striving to go beyond appearances to an honest confrontation with what following Christ demands of us in the face of new and unexpected challenges;
4. Coming to a kind of felt-knowledge (*sentir*) or an effective, intuitive knowing as to where the Spirit is leading us and whether certain decisions or actions will draw us closer to God's will or not; and
5. Making a final determination, in the light of the Gospel and according to ecclesial norms, to respond wholeheartedly to God's will as Jesus did, no matter the cost.

The end result of this process is a listening stance that renders us free and objective, able to view life with a contemplative eye and to act according to the command of love.

Ignatius of Loyola, Saint

(1491-1556) Founder of the Society of Jesus, Ignatius was the youngest son of a Basque nobleman. As a young man his dream was to be a soldier. During a long convalescence, following a siege in which he was wounded, he did much reading of the life of Christ and the saints. After a time he determined to give himself wholly to God's service, to be a soldier for Christ.

His **zeal** was unmatched as he exchanged the clothing of a dignitary for the rough garb of a beggar and pledged himself to the service of the

Blessed Virgin Mary. After a year's retirement at Manresa, he made a pilgrimage to Jerusalem. He was certain after this trip that God wanted him to be a priest. That meant continuing his education, which he did from 1524 to 1534, in Barcelona and at the University of Paris. In Paris he inspired seven students, among them **Saint Francis Xavier**, to vow to be missionaries to the Moslems in Palestine. Slowly the original members increased in numbers and—since war made it impossible for them to journey to Palestine—they offered their services to Pope Paul III.

At the age of forty-seven, Ignatius was ordained to the priesthood. Various tasks were assigned to him and the members of the group he called the Society of Jesus. Ignatius founded this religious order with the usual vows, but to them he added one more: to be at the pope's disposal and to serve the Church in whatever way she required. In 1540, he was elected the first Superior General of the Jesuits. His composition of the *Spiritual Exercises* guided the members of the Society in the art and discipline of discursive **meditation** as an avenue to **contemplative prayer**. His counsel to them summarizes the aim of his life: "I beseech you by the same Lord to make yourselves able to receive his visitation and spiritual treasures by **purity of heart** and genuine **humility** ... in a word, by your all being made completely one in our Lord Jesus Christ."

Illuminative Way (Illumination)
Commonly called in mystical theology the way of proficients, this middle stage of the spiritual journey can be distinguished from the **purgative** path of beginners that precedes it and the **unitive** way of the perfect that follows it. **Saint John of the Cross** in *The Dark Night* also refers to it as the way of infused **contemplation** insofar as God takes over totally, relieving our hunger and thirst for his presence without any intervening discursive meditations or active efforts. At these felt depths of friendship with the Divine, the Alone communicates with the alone, offering the soul food for the journey and validating Christ's promise to give us life, and life abundantly (John 10:10).

People more proficient in their response to grace move from a kind of courtship phase to one of spiritual betrothal. These illuminative lights are like foretastes of heaven on earth, but one must not cling to them inordinately, or new nights of the spirit may be sent by God to purify the soul more completely.

According to **Adrian van Kaam**, the many times we miss the mark despite purifying formation make us conscious of the shallow and vulnerable disposi-

> *Inspirations*
>
> My Lord, your mercy inspires me to suffer for your love and to imitate your life which was one continual martyrdom of suffering. Let me feel the desire to humble myself for love of you. Show me how to do this, since in many circumstances I almost don't feel the courage to follow your holy inspirations.
>
> –*Saint Frances Xavier Cabrini*

tions our pride-form mistakes for virtues. The latter need to be reformed many times over if true Christian dispositions are to become second nature to us. Our **consolation** is that we have at least caught a glimpse of the dawn.

Such a process of reformation follows no set schedule, but it does give us fresh insights and inner strength. It is as if we understand without understanding, as if we bask under the sun, enjoying its warmth and brightness without getting burnt. If purgation renders the complex simple, the impure pure, then illumination cleanses our palate of base tastes so that we can experience, if only for a brief duration, the sweet delights of divine love.

Irenaeus of Lyons, Saint

(c. 125-202) One of the early defenders of the faith against the heresy of gnosticism, Irenaeus was born and raised in Asia Minor. As bishop of Lyons, Irenaeus became a powerful voice in refuting the heretical claim that God is not fully incarnate in Christ. He believed that to the degree that we are created in God's image, we must be transformed into his likeness and thereby realize our potential for divine life ("deification") with all its stability, love, and freedom.

To his credit, Saint Irenaeus was the first Christian writer to point out that the purpose of God's sharing in human life is that humans might share in the life divine. To him is attributed the beautiful saying, "The glory of God is man fully alive."

Characteristic of Irenaeus' teaching is the Pauline emphasis on the love of God for us and on our call to share in the life of Jesus. In the saint's words, "The less God has need of anything, the more human beings need to be united with him. Consequently, a human being's true glory is to persevere in the service of God."

Jerome, Saint

(331-420) One of the most renowned Latin Fathers and Doctors of the Church, Jerome was also able, because of his knowledge of Greek, Hebrew, and Syrian, to bridge the gap between East and West, especially in the realms of biblical scholarship and the monasticism of the desert tradition.

As a student in Rome, Jerome was a tireless scholar, a gifted translator, and a skilled exegete. After Christ touched his heart in a vivid dream, he set aside his worldly ambitions to become a hermit in the desert. There he lived a life of self-sacrifice combined with a passion for reflection on the Word of God. The one possession he did not leave behind when he sought the hermit's life was his library. He saw **solitude** as an occasion to concentrate on his studies.

For Jerome **spiritual** reading (*lectio divina*) and **unceasing prayer** (*oratio*) are complementary endeavors. In the former exercise we listen to God, in the latter we speak to his heart. Jerome says of prayer: "Let [it] fortify us when we leave our lodgings. As we return from the streets, prayer should be offered before we sit down. Nor should our wretched body have rest before the soul is fed." The ascetic life facilitates this dialogue, as does commitment to **obedience, poverty,** and **chastity.**

Though he stood firmly by his beliefs and the rigorous morality they required, Jerome was kindly and sympathetic to his many correspondents and to all who came to him for help and **spiritual direction**. Uncompromising as he was in his judgments against opponents of the Church, Jerome was as prone to judge himself unworthy of the graces he received. In 382 he left his beloved desert retreat to return to Rome to serve as the secretary of Pope Damascus. In 385 he made a pilgrimage to the Holy Land and Egypt and decided to settle thereafter in Bethlehem. He lived in a cave near the site commemorating the birth of Jesus. He also founded a monastery for men and another for women, the latter being the home of Saints Marcella and Paula, who remained at his side and assisted in the mammoth work of biblical translation. When Paula died in 404, Jerome wrote that he had lost "her who was his consolation." Their work bore more fruit than either could have imagined: his Vulgate Bible was the official text of the Church for over fifteen hundred years.

Jesus Prayer

The Orthodox tradition of "hesy-chasm" (from the Greek *hesychia* or "quiet") centers on four main points:

1. Seeking a state of contemplative rest, excluding reading, psalmody, **meditation**, and other forms of **devotion;**
2. Repeating the "Jesus Prayer" ("Lord Jesus Christ, Son of God, have mercy on me, a sinner" or simply "Jesus, mercy"), allowing it to permeate both mind and heart;
3. Using practices designed to aid concentration, such as physical immobility, breath control, and focusing the eyes of the mind on the heart; and
4. Feeling at times inner warmth or perceiving an epiphanic radiance likened to the "light of Tabor."

Rather than multiplying thoughts and feelings, one endeavors to minimize them by returning to the prayer and letting **distractions** go by without words or arguments. In due course it is not we who pray the prayer; rather it prays itself in us.

In the Eastern Church, the practice of the Jesus Prayer is outlined in *The Philokalia, The Way of the Pilgrim,* and many other treatises that address the mystery and meaning of the name of Jesus. A contemporary exponent of this way of prayer, Kallistos Ware, has said that the invocation of Jesus' name, while being a prayer of utmost simplicity, accessible to every Christian, leads at the same time to the deepest mysteries of contemplation. The more this prayer becomes a part of our lives, "the more we enter into the movement of love which passes unceasingly between Father, Son, and Holy Spirit."

John Chrysostom, Saint

(354-407) The name of this master means "golden mouth," a title honoring him as one of the finest preachers in the early Church. He was born in Antioch, the son of a Roman general. His gifts for rhetoric and his interest in philosophy seemed to point toward a career in law, but John was drawn instead to the study of Scripture and theology. He was baptized in 368, and immediately thereafter began his four-year transformation through self-discipline and **asceticism**. He lived in **solitude**, first in his mother's home and then under the direction of an aged hermit, a Syrian monk, in a mountainous region near Antioch.

When his health failed, due in part to the severity of his ascetic life, John returned to the city; he was ordained a priest in 386. For the next twelve years he preached in the Cathedral of Antioch. As a pastor of souls, his eloquence and knowledge of the Scriptures, and his ability to connect them to daily life with an elegance of style enhanced by his knowledge of Greek literature, attracted many hearers to renewed love for God's word. He reminded his listeners, "If my words were held in your souls, with all certainty they would have kept you here in the Church and have sent you on to the awesome mysteries in a deep spirit of piety."

In 398 he was consecrated patriarch of Constantinople. Popular as he was as a preacher, John never lost the simplicity he found in solitude nor his **devotion** to the needs of the poor. As the years passed, he endured hatred and misunderstanding on the part of the empress, vilification by fellow clergy for his denunciation of their apathy and abuse of the clerical office, and even exile to Armenia. During this time he began to write influential letters to his friends, expressive of his courage and commitment to endure hardships for the love of God. Though the people of Antioch welcomed his return from exile, his political and ecclesiastical opponents continued to persecute him. They even made an attempt on his life and banished him from the empire once again. Exiled to a still remoter region, he died in 407. His works on the Hebrew Scriptures and the New Testament comprise several volumes. His treatise *On Priesthood* and his oft-quoted essay *On Virginity* confirm his conviction that "no matter where we happen to be, by prayer we can set up an altar to God in our heart."

John of the Cross, Saint

(1542-91) Acknowledged as one of the most renowned spiritual masters in the Western Church, Saint John knew the meaning of suffering from childhood on. His father died when he and his two brothers were young boys; then one of them, Luis, died, too. The other, Francisco, was sent to live with relatives, leaving John and his mother to find sustenance on their own. To help make ends meet in their hometown of Medina del Campo, John worked in an orphanage-hospital taking care of the poorest of the poor and, in the process, learning the meaning of **compassion** for humanity wounded by sickness and sin.

He entered the Carmelite community in 1564. After his novitiate he was sent to study at the University of Salamanca, where he completed his thesis on the theme of fidelity to the doctrine of the Church. This theme became the keynote of his life and led in due course to his being named a Doctor of the Church.

After his ordination in 1567, he met the woman who would change his life as he would change hers, **Saint Teresa of Avila**. She shared with the newly ordained friar her dream of reforming the Carmelite Order by returning to the original rule of Saint Albert. She would make the distinguishing feature of her reform the wearing of sandals, not shoes, to symbolize the **poverty** she wished her sisters to embrace. They would be known forthwith as the Discalced Carmelites.

John was so gripped by her vision that he sought **solitude** at an old farm in Duruelo, which became the first monastery of the Discalced friars. That same year, 1568, he conceded to Mother Teresa's request to open another house at Alba de Tórmes, which he practically built by hand. Being recognized as the first master and spiritual director of the Discalced Carmelites did not endear John to his order.

The "reformers" felt the hostility of the "traditionalists" from the start, even though the old group had allowed many mitigations to slip into the rule and its original **charism**. The wheels were set in motion, politically and ecclesially, to squelch the reform. In December of 1577, the saint entered what would truly be the dark night of his life. He was kidnapped and imprisoned in the convent at Toledo, where he endured a starvation diet, solitary confinement, and cruel beatings at the hands of his own brothers. Yet it was in this prison that he found his poetic voice, composing there the first of his great lyrics, *The Spiritual Canticle.*

Miraculously, about nine months later, Fra Juan escaped from his tiny cell and was led to safety, thanks to the help of the sisters. He composed his second poem, *The Dark Night*, shortly after this leap to freedom. Much as he longed for peace, the internal battles between the two branches of the order did not cease until June of 1580, when Pope Gregory XIII signed the documents officially declaring that the Discalced were a separate province within the order. Saint John was subsequently elected one of their provincial counselors. At the same time he continued to teach and help the sisters. He began as well a prolific writing career, consisting of the two poems that reflected his experience of God while he was in prison, his commentary on them, and his third lyric masterpiece, *The Living Flame of Love*, which was composed in a state of ecstasy in 1585. His poetry and prose works—perhaps the greatest ever written in the fields of ascetic and mystical theology–were completed during the last fourteen years of his life when his intellectual and spiritual gifts had come to full flower. He died as he had lived on December 14, 1591, happy to have drunk from the cup of Christ's own suffering and thereby, in his words, to have penetrated "deep into the thicket of the delectable wisdom of God."

Joy in God

A great fullness of spiritual comfort and joy in God comes into the hearts of those who recite or devoutly intone the psalms as an act of praise to Jesus Christ. They drop sweetness in men's souls and pour delight into their thoughts and kindle their wills with the fire of love, making them hot and burning within, and beautiful and lovely in Christ's eyes.

–*Richard Rolle*

Julian of Norwich

(c. 1342-73) This extraordinarily gifted fourteenth-century English mystic and solitary "anchoress" was devoted to prayer and **contemplation**. She lived simply yet comfortably in her "cell" attached to the Church of Saint Julian in Norwich, England. She was around thirty years old and in the throes of a near-fatal illness when she experienced a series of sixteen revelations or "showings," which included visions of Mary and Jesus and even the devil. For the rest of her life, Julian pondered the meaning of these visions.

Though little is known of Julian biographically, one thing is certain: she wrote her famous *Showings* or *Revelations of Divine Love* in a turbulent era, riddled with catastrophic events like the Black Plague, the Hundred Years' War, religious persecution, and a papal schism. Women were largely unrecognized in intellectual circles, but Julian's contributions were taken seriously, since the cloistered life gave her a voice commanding respect. Her incredible optimism has contributed to her reputation as one of the holiest and wisest of the English spiritual writers. Her work is lauded not only by scholars but also by the same common folk she loved and guided. Like us, they were people who questioned the meaning of life and their own approaching death. No wonder Julian's most quoted sentence has touched hearts over the ages: "All shall be well and all manner of things shall be well."

Despite the chaotic times in which Julian lived and wrote, she never failed to see the presence of God everywhere, even in something no bigger than a hazelnut. When she held this tiny bit of creation in the palm of her hand, Julian saw something of the nature of God, who made it, loves it, and preserves it as he does all of us, his children. Julian's authentic visions included the recollection of Christ's passion in vivid, even frightening detail; the meaning of suffering and bodily sickness, beheld in the light of God's fatherly and motherly goodness; and the sight of three wounds that imprinted the passion of Christ on our souls, these being contrition, compassion, and the longing for God.

Julian contrasts the horror of sin with the happiness that is ours as recipients of divine **mercy**. With the certitude of one who has seen the Christ who redeemed us, she knew of his desire to be united with us. She also introduced the notion of Jesus as our true Mother. In celebrating the tenderness of his humanity and the saving grace of his divinity, Julian was convinced that love, not sin, is the ultimate determinant of our existence. In both the short and the long form of her book, she affirms the goodness of creation, the friendship of Christ, and the sweet solicitude of the **Blessed Trinity**.

Justice

The *Catechism* defines justice as "the moral virtue that consists in the constant and firm will to give their due to God and neighbor" [1807]. This virtue, along with prudence, fortitude, and temperance, is a pivotal disposition around which many other human and moral goods can be grouped. It is, therefore, a cardinal virtue, rooted in Holy Scripture and in our Judeo-Christian faith and formation tradition.

To practice the "virtue of religion" is to show justice to God, who deserves our love, adoration, and awe. To do justice to our neighbors is to respect their personal, civil, and social rights; it is to uphold every form of human dignity from birth to death, to promote sound human relationships, and to bolster the conditions necessary for living the common good. Therefore, "commutative justice" regulates exchanges between persons calling for respect for their property rights, payment of debts owed to them, and the fulfilling of contractual obligations; "legal justice" concerns what a citizen owes to his or her community in all fairness; and "distributive justice" regulates in turn what a community owes its citizens [2411].

> ### *Know the Creed*
>
> I want a laity ... who know their religion and who enter into it, who know just where they stand, who know what they hold, and what they do not, who know their creed so well that they can give an account of it, who know so much history that they can defend it. I want an intelligent, well-instructed laity. I wish you to enlarge your knowledge, to cultivate your reason, to get an insight into the relation of truth, to learn to view things as they are, to understand how faith and reason stand to each other, what are the bases and principles of Catholicism.
>
> —*John Henry Cardinal Newman*

Kolbe, Saint Maximilian
(1894-1941) This future saint, whose life was not without controversy, seemed to be destined for the priesthood from the moment of his birth in Poland. His mother, Maria, had wanted to enter the convent, but when circumstances made this impossible she was blessed to find in her husband, Julius, a God-fearing man who shared her **devotion** to the Blessed Mother. Together they conveyed their love for Mary Immaculate to their middle son, whose baptismal name was Raymond, and to his brothers Joseph and Francis.

Raymond received the gift of being called to the priesthood for which his mother had prayed. He entered the Order of Saint Francis, where he received his habit in 1900, along with a new name, Maximilian Maria. By 1914, he had completed his studies at the College of the Conventual Franciscans, and on November 1 of that year, pronounced his solemn vows. A year later he earned his doctorate in philosophy at the Gregorian University.

In 1917 Maximilian made a decisive discovery. During his **meditation** on January 20 of that year, he understood the inspiration that he was to organize an association that would be dedicated to the service of the **Blessed Virgin Mary**. Its aim would be to help all people through her intercession to gain full liberation from sin and total transformation in Christ. This lofty goal would be realized with his founding of the Knights of the Immaculata in Rome. This work would occupy him for the rest of his life.

By 1929 the Knights numbered

250,000 members and were spread as far as India and Japan. At its peak over 800,000 copies of their monthly newsletter were in circulation in many languages. All credit for this expansion was given to Mary and the dogma of her Immaculate Conception. His Queen's *fiat* soon enough became the only operable word on Kolbe's lips.

The Nazis determined to suppress his voice and the powerful message of love and freedom in the Lord it sounded over the radio and in print. The war machine that sought to obliterate the Jewish people overtook Father Maximilian himself in 1939, when he and thirty-six of his friars were arrested and deported to different concentration camps. Gestapo officers tried to beat Kolbe into renouncing his faith, but to no avail. As a final act of selfless love, Maximilian offered to take the place of one man, a husband and father, who along with nine others had been condemned to die as payment for an escaped prisoner the Gestapo had not recaptured. Having lasted for four weeks without food or water, this holy martyr received a fatal injection on August 14, 1941. He died as he had lived, with courage and complete dedication to Jesus and Mary.

Kowalska, Saint Maria Faustina (1905-38) This modern-day mystic and proponent of the **devotion** to Divine Mercy grew up in a poor farming family in Poland during the devastation caused by the First World War. She had only three years of formal education, yet Jesus chose her, as she reveals in her diary, to be his "secretary"—the one through whom his message of **mercy** would be revealed to the world.

Faustina entered the Congregation of the Sisters of Our Lady of Mercy in Cracow, Poland, and was assigned to do the humblest chores, working in the convent kitchen and tending the vegetable garden. On February 22, 1931, Christ appeared to this simple sister and revealed a glorious image of himself. The now-famous revelation was recorded on that date in Faustina's diary as follows:

> In the evening, when I was in my cell, I became aware of the Lord Jesus clothed in a white garment. One hand was raised in blessing, the other was touching the garment at the breast. From the opening in the garment at the breast there came forth two large rays, one red, and the other pale. In silence I gazed intently at the Lord; my soul was overwhelmed with fear, but also with great joy. After a while Jesus

> said to me: "Paint an image according to the pattern you see, with the inscription: Jesus, I trust in You."

Later the Lord explained to Faustina what the image meant. "The pale ray," he said, "stands for the water which makes souls righteous; the red ray stands for the Blood which is the life of souls. These two rays issued forth from the depths of My most tender Mercy at that time when My agonizing Heart was opened by a lance on the Cross … Fortunate is the one who will dwell in their shelter, for the just hand of God shall not lay hold of him." Jesus also asked his "little secretary" to issue a call to the whole Church to celebrate the Feast of Divine Mercy on the first Sunday after Easter, for on that day he would open the depths of his mercy to all.

Perhaps no one needed these touches of consolation and compassion more than Faustina herself. During her lifetime she had to endure the crosses of misunderstanding and persecution, even by the members of her own community. For many years after her death, a wall of silence surrounded her work due to its being inaccurately presented to the Holy See. Finally, in April of 1978, after thorough examination of the original documents, the Vatican, under the jurisdiction of Karol Cardinal Wojtyla, Archbishop of Cracow (later Pope John Paul II), reversed its decision and upheld the devotion to Divine Mercy outlined in Faustina's diary. In 1992, through Faustina's intercession, a miracle of healing occurred. This event, together with her life of heroic virtue, allowed the pope to declare this apostle of Divine Mercy "Blessed" as the first step to her canonization by him on Divine Mercy Sunday, April 30, 2000.

L

Ladder of Charity

Was it not a foretaste of blessedness thus to love and thus to be loved; thus to help and thus to be helped; and in this way from the sweetness of fraternal charity to wing one's flight aloft to that more sublime splendor of divine love, and by the ladder of charity now to mount to the embrace of Christ himself; and again to descend to the love of neighbor, there pleasantly to rest?

–Saint Aelred of Rievaulx

Lawrence of the Resurrection, Brother

(1611-91) Born in the Lorraine region of France, Nicholas Herman served in the army and worked as a household employee before deciding in middle age to enter the Discalced Carmelite order. There he assumed his new name, Brother Lawrence, but remained a humble worker, enjoying his kitchen duties and cobbler tasks for the next forty years and learning the wisdom that comes with increasing **prayer**.

Abbé Joseph de Beaufort, who had often visited the monk before his death, published a memoir in Brother Lawrence's name based on their conversations as well as sixteen of Brother Lawrence's letters and some of his spiritual maxims. *Practicing the Presence of God* would become a Christian classic. In it we learn in simple yet profound terms that **faith** in the midst of everyday events brings us to a high degree of perfection, whether or not special feelings accompany our quest for holiness.

Brother Lawrence's way of **spiritual childhood** was so simple anyone could follow it, with or without the help of a spiritual director. His "shortcut to God" consisted not of traditional methods of prayer and ascetic practices but of the continual practice of love and doing everything for the Beloved with **humility** and reverence. *Forget about the past. Do not worry about the future,* he counseled others. *Live in the present and count on God to give you whatever you need when you need it.*

Brother Lawrence's approach to prayer was simple yet profound: Do everything for God's sake and don't get discouraged when small tests come your way. Adhere to God in labor and leisure, and cultivate the sense of his presence. In due course prayer will become as natural to you as breath. As he wrote to a priest, "I keep myself in his presence by simple attentiveness and a general loving awareness of God that I call 'actual presence of God' or better, a quiet and secret conversation of the soul with God that is lasting." Recognized as a spiritual guide by religious and laity alike, Brother Lawrence lived an exemplary life and died a holy death at the age of eighty.

Libermann, Venerable Francis

(1802-52) Cofounder, with Claude Poullard Des Places, of the Congregation of the Holy Ghost (the Spiritans), Jacob Libermann was born in Alsace, the son of a Jewish rabbi. His father had hoped at least one of his sons would choose his vocation; under his father's strict tutelage, Jacob and his brothers studied Talmudic law and were forbidden all but the most necessary contact with the outside world. His father's dreams were dashed, however, as one after the other of his four sons joined the Catholic Church.

At **Baptism**, Jacob took the name Francis and soon thereafter entered the seminary in Paris. Despite his good will and pious spirit, he was physically handicapped by headaches, dizzy spells, speech impediments, and, worst of all, epilepsy. Yet God chose this weakest of men to be an epiphany of Christ-centered living. His fellow seminarians were uplifted by his humble acceptance of God's will and his affectionate concern for the less fortunate.

His reliable reputation as a holy and compassionate spiritual guide confirmed his call to the priesthood, but Francis' persistent poor health delayed his ordination. No matter. He left all in the hands of God and devoted his time to solitary prayer, writing, and good works, while starting to dream about a new missionary order that would be dedicated to serving the most abandoned souls. Africa occupied a special place in his heart; however, no soul in educational or spiritual need would be forgotten.

Following his ordination, Francis received permission to start the Congregation of the Holy Heart of Mary. He told the men who joined him that they had to counter the romantic desire that missionary work meant martyrdom. He urged them to take every precaution and to prefer effective efforts to erratic heroism. Even so, many early missionaries were lost. Libermann insisted on the rule of moderation in all things and the embracing of God's will.

Intuition tempered by practicality led before long to the decision to merge his new order with the already existing Congregation of the Holy Ghost, though as in any merger this one too required diplomacy, serenity, and **humility**—all traits in which this venerable cofounder excelled. In the twelve years in which he lived after his ordination, Francis bore again the cross of poor health though his output of work was prodigious, resulting in volumes of letters to priests and people in the world. His spirit lives on in the worldwide mission network of Spiritans, who continue to serve the physically and spiritually oppressed and disadvantaged from every walk of life—particularly in those places the Church has difficulty recruiting workers.

Liguori, Saint Alphonsus

(1696-1787) A native of Naples and the son of distinguished parents, Liguori displayed such outstanding intellectual gifts that he became a doctor of civil law by his seventeenth birthday. His love for the priesthood prevailed over a secular career. Soon after his ordination in 1726, he received accolades as a preacher and was eagerly sought as a confessor.

Alphonsus wanted to preach sermons that were simple yet profound, doctrinally sound yet practical, well structured yet able to hold people's attention. His concern for educating and forming souls led him to found an order of missionary priests named the Redemptorists. His famous book, *Moral Theology* (1748), became a standard text in seminary education. A kind and generous man, a true shepherd of souls, Alphonsus became a bishop in 1762. He was named a Doctor of the Church in 1871.

Liturgy

The supreme act of worship in our faith tradition is to celebrate the liturgy. Here the people of God participate in a special way in the work of God. As we learn in the *Catechism*, "Through the liturgy Christ, our redeemer and high priest, continues the work of our redemption in, with, and through his Church" [1069].

The word "liturgy" is used in two ways in the New Testament. In one sense, this word refers to the celebration of divine worship; it also refers to the proclamation of the gospel and to the practice of **charity**. The liturgy expresses at one and the same time the first and second parts of the Great Commandment: to love God with our whole being, and to love our neigh**bor** as we love ourselves.

Liturgy is also an action of the Church, which, in the words of the *Catechism*, "makes [her] present and manifests her as a visible sign of the communion in Christ between God and men" [1071]. Liturgy is not like a staged performance viewed passively from our seats; it is meant to engage the faithful in the life of the **faith** community, in the work of evangelization, prayer, and ongoing **conversion**. In the words of Pope John Paul II cited in the *Catechism*:

> The Church and the world have a great need for Eucharistic worship. Jesus awaits us in this sacrament of love. Let us not refuse the time to go to meet him in adoration, in contemplation full of faith, and open to making amends for the serious offenses and crimes of the world. Let our adoration never cease [1380].[1]

Liturgy of the Hours

Also known as the Divine Office, this practice contains the official daily and public prayers of the Church, consisting of morning (Lauds) and evening (Vespers), daytime prayers (Terce, Sext, and None), and night prayers (Matins), along with scriptural and sacred readings, all designed and selected to help the Church to follow the apostolic injunction to pray unceasingly.

The roots of the Divine Office can be found in the practice of the early Christians, who patterned their formal prayer life on Jewish Temple worship with a view toward preparing people for the celebration of the Mass and other feast days. The present office is traceable to early Christian monastic life as exemplified in **Benedictine Spirituality**. In the Latin Church clerics in sacred orders have the obligation of saying the Divine Office, at least privately, an obligation shared by men and women in solemn vows in religious and monastic life.

According to the *Catechism,* reverential, regular celebration of the Liturgy of the Hours is an exemplary way in which Christ-in-us continues his priestly work in the Church. The Office has a special place in the life of priests and religious, and yet laity also have become increasingly attracted to its classical beauty and devotional splendor, its sanctification of the time of day and the liturgical seasons.

Lord's Prayer

When the disciples asked Jesus to teach them to pray (Luke 11:1), he gave them a prayer that the Church Father Tertullian aptly called a "summary of the whole gospel." This prayer consists of seven petitions. The first three focus on God and his glory: May his name be hallowed, may his kingdom come, may his will be done.

In the first of these petitions, we give God the primacy of place in our lives, which is his due. By implication, we express our **call to holiness** and our **hope** that people will fulfill with joy their obligation to venerate God with awe and reverence. In the second petition, we remember our need for ongoing **conversion** marked by the commitment to serve God's reign in the world. The third petition is the most difficult one for us to say, yet it is the most urgent. Our food must become, as Jesus' was, the will of the Father and the willingness to do his work (John 4:34). **Abandonment to Divine Providence** means that we say "yes" to the Father as the foundation and ultimate meaning of our existence. This "yes" is our response to the love of God that precedes us, as well as the grace that follows us and enables our salvation.

The last four petitions of the Lord's Prayer focus on our concerns: to be given our daily bread, to be forgiven as we forgive others, to not be led into temptation, and to be delivered from evil. The Bread of Life that we receive in the **Eucharist** as well as the food on our table remind us to place our trust in God. He answers our needs spiritually and materially, but we have to do our part in **justice** to share our bread with the world.

The petition pertaining to **forgiveness** makes clear that we are sinners in need of redemption. The barely noticeable word "as" in the phrase, "as we forgive those who trespass against us," further suggests that divine **mercy** can penetrate our hearts only if we are willing to share God's forgiveness of us with others. Without a forgiving heart it is difficult, if not impossible, to pray as Jesus does, since there is no limit or measure to divine forgiveness and the Father's offer of reconciliation with sinners. To consent to the Spirit's leading gives us the strength to resist temptation. Moreover, as we know from Scripture, God will not test us beyond our strength; he will give us the grace we need to endure (cf. 1 Corinthians 10:13).

Christ's power is such that he liberates us continually from evil and sin, yet the struggle against evil ought never to be taken lightly. Each Christian has a fundamental role to play in this regard. That is why with the whole Church we pray at Mass, following the recitation of the Our Father: "Deliver us, Lord, we beseech you, from every evil and grant us peace in our day, so that aided by your mercy we might be ever free from sin and protected from all anxiety, as we await the blessed **hope** and the coming of our Savior, Jesus Christ."

1. *Dominicae cenae* 3.

Marie of the Incarnation, Blessed (1599-1672) Growing up in a middle-class family in Tours, France, Marie aspired to enter the religious life. However, she had to obey her parents' wishes that she marry at the age of seventeen. Two years later her husband died, leaving her with their young son to raise. She was forced to earn their keep as a servant in the home of her brother-in-law. In 1620 she received a life-changing revelation of the **mercy** of God that portended other great visions she would receive from 1625 onward.

By 1631 Marie at last entered the novitiate of the Ursuline nuns near her hometown of Tours. Though her son, did not take this news lightly, since it meant that he would have to continue living with their in-laws, he eventually changed his mind and himself became a Benedictine and the author of his mother's biography.

In 1639 Marie and another young sister started an Ursuline foundation in Quebec, Canada, where she was to spend the rest of her life as an educator. Her influence on the Indian population there was great. To serve her mission more fully, she mastered three of their languages: Algonquin, Iroquois, and Huron.

In the midst of her apostolic endeavors, at her confessor's request Marie kept accurate records of her spiritual progress and her mystical experiences, utilizing in her description the language and distinctions made in the collected works of **Saint Teresa of Avila** and **Saint John of the Cross**. In the most systematic account of her spiritual life, she was able to distinguish the stages of spiritual betrothal, courtship, and marriage and to see mirrored in her soul the life of the **Blessed Trinity**. As she writes: "When my soul received this illumination it understood and experienced at the same time how it was created to the image of God: that the memory relates it to the eternal Father, the understanding to the Son, and the will to the Holy Spirit; and that, just as the most Holy Trinity is threefold in Persons but one in essence, so also the soul is threefold in its powers but one in its substance."

Mary, Blessed Virgin
From the moment she uttered her courageous *fiat,* Mary became the chief collaborator in the work her Son was sent to accomplish. For this reason, the *Catechism* teaches that the "Marian" dimension of the Church precedes the "Petrine" [773].

All the mysteries of her life are meditated upon in the rosary: the joyful events of the annunciation, of her visitation to her cousin Elizabeth, of the Incarnation itself on that wondrous first Christmas Eve. A sense of the hardship she would have to endure came during the presentation of Jesus in the temple and later when she found him teaching among the scribes and Pharisees and learned that the time would come when he would have to be wholly about his Father's business. It was she who helped to initiate his public life at the wedding feast at Cana when, at her request, he changed water into wine.

The sorrowful mysteries depict the unspeakable grief that must have been hers when she saw her beloved Son, after his agony in the garden, scourged at the pillar, crowned with thorns, and made to carry his own cross. But she never left his side. She was there with the other women at the foot of the cross, and she received his body into her arms when he died on Calvary.

She was with the apostles in that upper room on the first Pentecost day and, after the Ascension of her Son, she "aided the beginnings of the Church by her prayers."[1] Finally, this virgin, preserved from all stain of original sin, was taken up body and soul into heaven and "exalted by the Lord as Queen over all things ..." [966].

Marian **devotion** is intrinsic to Christian worship, for "she shines forth on earth, until the day of the Lord shall come, a sign of certain hope and comfort to the pilgrim people of God."[2]

Maximus the Confessor, Saint

(c. 580-662) Called the last great theologian of Greek patristics, Maximus is one of the most profound mystics of the Eastern Church. It is thought that Maximus grew up in a distinguished family in Constantinople and became a secretary of the emperor until he entered a monastery near Carthage in 613. Other traditions say he was born in Palestine and lived there as a monk before coming to Constantinople. In any case, Maximus came under the influence of the patriarch of Jerusalem. There and in Alexandria his brilliance as a defender of the **faith** became apparent, making him the target of persistent animosity.

Though he was mainly concerned with mystical, exegetical, and liturgical matters, as exemplified in his *Commentary on the "Our Father"* (c. 640) and *The Church's Mystagogy* (c. 625), Maximus spent most of his energy in the defense of orthodox doctrine against heretical claims that there was a separation of the divine and human nature of God in the second Person of the **Blessed Trinity**. An example particularly offensive to Maximus was monophysitism, which denied the humanity of Christ. According to this heresy, he had only one nature, and that was divine. Monothelitism, another heresy Maximus fought, insisted that Christ had a divine will but not a human will.

In addition to his dogmatic and polemic writings, Maximus expounded a doctrine of **charity**, centering on the love of Christ, our Incarnate Redeemer. One of his best-known works is the *Four Hundred Chapters on Love.* In it he shows that it is charity that deifies the soul and enables us to experience our "adoptive filiation" in the family of the Trinity, a relationship ultimately realized in that wholly graced bond of union with God that is mystical marriage or, in a description preferred by the Greek Fathers, "deification."

Maximus paid a high price for his faith. In 662, he was imprisoned in Constantinople where the same heretics he castigated condemned him to be scourged and to have his tongue cut off, and his right hand amputated as a symbol of his commitment as a "confessor" or witness to the true faith. He died that same year, having proclaimed Christ's praises and suffered persecution for his sake. He is revered in the East and the West as a saint and a Doctor of the Church.

Mechthild of Magdeburg

(c. 1260-c. 1282) A German mystic, visionary, and member of the Beguines (a thirteenth-century women's movement in Germany, Belgium, and the Netherlands), Mechthild strove to fashion a new form of religious life that would become a haven for women like herself, who wanted to live a simple existence of common prayer, manual labor, and service to the poor. Gifted with a flare for spiritual guidance, combined with the courage of prophecy, Mechthild took the time to plot the entire course of her inner journey in her now famous book, *The Flowing Light of the Godhead.* As she discloses:

> ... a great light appeared to my soul, and in this light God revealed himself in great majesty and indescribable brightness. Our Lord held two golden chalices in his hands that were both full of living wine. In his left hand was the red wine of suffering, and in his right hand the white wine of sublime **consolation**. Then our Lord spoke: "Blessed are those who drink this red wine. Although I give both out of divine love, the white wine is nobler in itself; but noblest of all are those who drink both the white and the red!"

In her writings Mechthild commingles mystical love poetry, dialogues with Christ, accounts of her visions of heaven and hell, and unsparing criticism of ecclesial corruption. For the last half of her life she sought and found refuge in the Cistercian convent of Helfta, where two other mystics, **Saint Gertrude the Great** and Mechthild of Hackeborn, welcomed her and cared for her until she died. She is a woman of such **faith** that for her death had no sting. It was the ultimate entrance to divine intimacy. In her words, "Give me, Lord, and take from me, Lord, everything you want, and leave me just this wish—that I might die of love in love. Amen."

Meditation

Meditation or meditative reflection is a combined exercise of the imaginative, cognitive, and affective faculties of the mind to seek the meaning of what God may be saying through a particular event or passage in a text. To meditate is to reflect with regularity upon the Word of God, on our response or resistance to God's will, and on our calling in this life. This reflection is not an external exercise that relies on grappling with new information but an internal process of ruminating on the text or narrative at hand with the intention of connecting its meaning to the **will of God.** To meditate is to discover the Word of God not only in the background of our Christian life but also in the foreground of our person-to-Person encounters with the living God.

Such a style of reading and reflecting on what we read helps us to assess our failings as well as to affirm our gifts. In these moments of dwelling on the Word, we may sense God's self-communication to us. The Holy Spirit can and does use times like these to draw us along the paths of prayer, **contemplation**, and Christian action.

Meditation prevents our ministry from degenerating into mere activism that exhausts us and in the end becomes offensive to others. This practice encourages us to face life's ultimate meaning rather than to fall into dull routine, burying ourselves in sheer functionalism or losing our self-respect in wanton gratification. Uplifted by the wisdom of the masters, meditators can walk the way of the Lord and become an epiphany of his presence in the world.

Mercy

We imitate God's compassionate response to us when we practice two forms of mercy, corporal and spiritual. The seven works of corporal mercy address the physical well-being of needy persons: to feed the hungry, to clothe the naked, to give drink to the thirsty, to console the sick, to visit prisoners, to give shelter to strangers, and to bury the dead. The core disposition of the heart behind these acts of mercy is **compassion** in the face of others' destitution and vulnerability. It tempers the strict demands of **justice** and, therefore, makes mercy an extension of the virtue of **charity**.

The spiritual works of mercy are another way we imitate the outflow of God's own compassion for us. These acts of love are addressed to persons in need not only of bodily but also of spiritual sustenance. The seven works are: to instruct the ignorant, to counsel the doubtful, to comfort the sorrowful, to admonish the sinner, to forgive injuries, to bear injustices patiently, and to pray for the living and the dead.

In our day a great **devotion** to Divine Mercy has sprung up thanks to the writings of **Saint Maria Faustina Kowalska**. Her diary contains many revelations concerning this **devotion**, among them these words of Jesus recorded by his "secretary" on September 14, 1937: "My Daughter, do you think you have written enough about My mercy? What you have written is but a drop compared to the ocean. I am Love and Mercy itself. There is no misery that could be a match for My mercy, neither will misery exhaust it, because as it is being granted—it increases. The soul that trusts in My mercy is most fortunate, because I myself take care of it."

Merici, Saint Angela

(1474-1540) A native of Brecia, Italy, and foundress of the Ursulines, Saint Angela embraced Lady Poverty in the spirit of **Saint Francis of Assisi**. Orphaned at the age of ten, she became a Franciscan tertiary in her teens. She understood from experience the need of the poor for a decent education. Along with a few friends, she began to instruct girls in an early version of home schooling.

Placing their religious association under the protection of Saint Ursula, patroness of medieval university education, the consecrated women wore no habit, and neither took solemn vows nor lived in a community. And yet four years after the death of their foundress, the Company of Saint Ursula was officially recognized by the Church. Its daughters would include many dedicated and holy women, including **Blessed Marie of the Incarnation**, pioneers in the field of education and witnesses to **poverty of spirit**.

Merton, Thomas

(1915-68) A native of France, Merton traveled between his homeland and

America during the first years of his life. His mother died of cancer when he was six, and when Merton was ten his father brought him to Europe to live. He was enrolled subsequently in French and English schools, matriculating in 1933 from Clare College, Cambridge. In 1934 Merton returned to live permanently in the United States, taking graduate courses at Columbia, where the tireless activist became a popular figure on campus.

In 1938 Merton converted to Catholicism, an event that changed his life. Soon thereafter, he applied for admission to the Franciscan order, but, due to his recent conversion, he was asked to detain his novitiate and put his call to the test of time. Though crushed, he accepted the decision with courage, vowing that if he could not live in a monastery he would become a monk in the world. He taught English at Saint Bonaventure University and worked for a while with Catherine de Hueck Doherty in a settlement house in Harlem.

In 1941 he gave up teaching and followed his true call to be a Trappist monk at the Abbey of Gethsemani, Kentucky. From then on his life was a rhythm of prayer, work, and publication, including the autobiography that brought him fame, *The Seven Storey Mountain.*

Merton made solemn vows in 1947 and became an American citizen in 1951. He was appointed to the position of Master of Novices in 1955, a post he held until 1965, when he obtained permission from his abbot to live as a hermit in a wooded area about a mile from the main buildings. There he sought to let go of other preoccupations and to plunge into the divine abyss wherein God's love encircles and takes possession of one's intellect, imagination, and will. Merton saw that we become contemplatives to the extent that we participate in Christ's divine Sonship. This, he says, is "God's greatest gift to the soul. It is a deep and intimate knowledge of God by a union of love—a union in which we learn things about him that those who have not received such a gift will never discover until they enter heaven."

Merton spent most of the remaining three years of his life in his hermitage. In the fall of 1968, he embarked on an extensive trip to the Far East to attend a conference on monasticism in Bangkok and to visit several Trappist monasteries. He gave a morning talk at the conference on aspects of Marxism and monasticism, but he never survived the day. On December 10, 1968, at the age of fifty-three, he was accidentally electrocuted by a defective fan.

Above all, Merton was a man of **faith**, a person of almost limitless expansiveness, whose writings witness to the truth that "there is no contradiction between action and **contemplation** when Christian apostolic activity is raised to the level of pure **charity**. On that level, action and contemplation are fused into one entity by the love of God and of our brother in Christ."

More, Saint Thomas

(1478-1535) The son of a lawyer and judge, Thomas More studied law at Oxford and entered Parliament as a respected, enlightened man, known by all as a good husband, the father of three daughters, and a deeply committed Catholic. Soon the king requested his services at Court where he became, somewhat reluctantly, Lord Chancellor to Henry VIII.

Thomas resigned three years later in opposition to the king's designs for successors to the throne. When this upright Christian refused to accept Henry's Act of Succession, he was arrested and imprisoned in the Tower of London. He went to his death nine days after Saint John Fisher met the same fate. In letters of **consolation,** penned to his family, he avowed that he was "the King's good servant, but God's first."

Mysticism

This word is synonymous with what **Saint John of the Cross** calls "mystical theology" or, more simply, the "science of love." In *The Dark Night,* he

Mighty and Merciful God

Hear me, good and great Lord,
for my soul hungers and longs
to feed upon the experience of your love,
but it cannot fill itself with you;
for my heart can find no name to invoke
that will satisfy my heart.
For no words have here any taste to me
when my love receives from you that which you give.
I have prayed, Lord, as I can,
but I wish I could do more.
Hear me, and answer as you are able,
for you can do all that you will,
I have prayed as a weak man and a sinner;
you who are mighty and merciful, hear my prayer.

–Saint Anselm of Canterbury

explains this favor as "an infused loving knowledge that both illumines and enamors the soul, elevating it step by step unto God, its Creator."

Mysticism must never be misunderstood as self-induced transcendent feelings or "spiritual highs." It is more like the secret disclosures of his divinity God gave to Moses on Mount Sinai (cf. Exodus 34:29). All one knows is that one has been brought by a favor beyond all deserving into the radiant light of the Mystery, an experience which leaves one stammering to find words to describe it.

What distinguishes authentic from inauthentic mysticism is that a true mystic stands for support on the solid foundation of **asceticism**. The instruction given to him or her may be wordless and without any feeling whatsoever, yet in the substance of the soul one is aware that a distinct change has taken place. This infusion of mystical graces produces three main effects in the soul.

According to Saint John, the first is preparatory or **purgative**, the second is reformative or **illuminative**, the third is transformative or **unitive**, though even on this third step our ability to understand the deep things of God is always an inability to do so.

Around such a relationship of intimacy with the **Blessed Trinity** there remains a residue of utter transcendence—what mystical theologians traditionally name the "apophatic way" or the "way of unknowing." In the words of Saint John of the Cross, "the brightest light in God is complete darkness to our intellect." Masters like **Saint Thomas Aquinas, Pseudo-Dionysius,** and the author of ***The Cloud of Unknowing*** confirm that such experiences are always beyond our best attempts to analyze them with strict logical accuracy. Still their fruits are unmistakable as one lives more and more in conformity to Christ, whose Paschal Mystery is the wellspring of all Christian mysticism.

1. LG 69.
2. LG 68; cf. 2 Pet 3:10.

N

Neri, Saint Philip

(1515-95) One of the leading figures in the spiritual revival of Catholicism in the sixteenth century, Neri felt led by God to pursue a life of prayer characterized by simplicity and ascetical fervor. With his confessor, Persiano Rosa, Neri decided to start a confraternity dedicated to the Trinity to help the poor on pilgrimage to Rome.

In 1551 he received the grace of Holy Orders. With his strong yet gentle personality and his obvious spiritual gifts, he began to attract a following of like-minded disciples, at first all laymen, who met with him on a daily basis for **spiritual reading**, **meditation**, and prayer.

After the ordination of a number of them in 1564, the inspiration came to Neri to found the Congregation of the Oratory, known for its **charism** of **spiritual direction**, complemented by frequent confession and communion—the very means Neri used to bind penitents and pilgrims to God. The members of the Congregation would be secular priests. They would stay together in small family-like groups with a certain **Benedictine** stability and a rich liturgical tradition. Their doors would always be open to the laity who sought to deepen their lives in interior prayer while maintaining their commitments in the world. He would often say, "Be humble and obedient and the Holy Spirit will teach you how to pray."

Neri's counsels included an appeal to mortify oneself inwardly through acts of love rather than engaging in austere practices lacking the lightheartedness of the children of God. He himself had no qualms about being a fool for Christ!

Another practice of his was to meditate on the **Lord's Prayer**, petition by petition. To keep God at the center of our lives, he urged the use of short ejaculations. When the souls he directed were in need of **consolation** due to the **aridity** of their prayer life, he counseled them to pick up an empty bowl and to carry it in their imagination from saint to saint, begging alms. So powerful was Neri's love for God and service to the sick in spirit and body that he became known in his lifetime as the "Apostle of Rome."

Never Stop Praying

It behooves us to pray hard so that all our mortal members with their powers—eyes, ears, heart, mouth, and all their senses—are turned in that direction, and we must never stop until we find ourselves on the point of union with him we have in mind and [to whom we] are praying, namely God.

–Meister Eckhart

Newman, John Henry Cardinal (1801-90) Cardinal Newman is a traditional Churchman in the fullest sense of this term. He embodies the Victorian sensibility for grace and good manners and the Anglican commitment to learning, expressed in the leading role he played in the Oxford Movement, which was dedicated to promoting the spiritual revival of the Church of England.

Newman attributed his own formation to the influence of the Anglican Divines, to people like Jeremy Taylor and Thomas Traberne, as well as to the Fathers of the Church, notably **Saint Athanasius of Alexandria,** from whom he derived his sense of the indwelling Trinity in the heart of every baptized soul.

Concerning his call to enter the Catholic Church, Newman said that was where the light had been leading him amidst, in his words, "the encircling gloom." The gloom dissipated much to his surprise when, in studying to find distortions in Catholic doctrine, he came to the opposite conclusion: that he himself should become a Catholic. Though his fellow Anglicans met his choice with sheer disbelief, he could not deny his call. Later in his book *The Grammar of Assent*, he would show that such a decision does not follow the laws of logic. It is a gift of pure **faith**.

Respected both by his peers and the common people as a scholar, a teacher, and a priest, Newman was also a prolific author. In his Anglican days, he delivered and published *Parochial and Plain Sermons*, which spoke in down-to-earth terms of the spiritual problems people face every day. It is not surprising that his call to serve eventually led him to the Oratory of **Saint Philip Neri**, whose love for the laity of every class appealed to Newman's sense of integrating the communal and unique lives of average Christians with liturgical and seasonal **worship**. He also emphasized the **Eucharist** the focal point of Christian prayer.

After becoming a priest of the Oratory, Newman accepted an invitation to go to Dublin to establish a Catholic institute of higher learning, which led to the writing of his masterpiece, *The Idea of a University.* The book brought him unsought notoriety and the ire of certain factions of the English Church with whose extreme conservative position Newman could not agree. He resisted labels like liberal or conservative in favor of right reason and balance. He was also ahead of his time in promoting the involvement of the laity in the Church. Newman preferred dialogue to stubborn debate, the assumption of individual moral responsibility to blind compliance with authority.

So respected was the role he played in reestablishing the Catholic Church in England that Pope Leo XIII named Newman a cardinal. Standing on the threshold of the modern era, Newman put his weight on the shoulders of tradition. He resisted close-minded conservatism as much as indiscriminate liberalism. He saw the intellectual life as the rich fruit of the spiritual life, and taught that "prayer is to the spiritual life what the beating of the pulse and the drawing of the breath are to the life of the body." It is significant that Pope Paul VI recognized the value of the cardinal's spirit of tolerance and integrity when he said of Vatican II that it was "Newman's Council."

Nicholas of Cusa, Bishop

(1401-64) An outstanding German intellectual, an effective ecclesiastical lawyer, and a consultant for East-West Church councils, Nicholas has been called the principal gatekeeper between medieval and modern philosophy. His theology of spirituality, rich in **mysticism**, is captured in such books as *On Learned Ignorance; On the Hidden God; On Seeking God; On the Vision of God;* and *On the Summit of Contemplation.* These books not only recall the brilliant influence of **Pseudo-Dionysius;** they also anticipate contemporary questions of ecumenicity and pluralism, empowerment and reconciliation, tolerance and respect for uniqueness, inclusivity versus exclusivity.

Nicholas draws us time and again into the exciting orbit of a benevolent God, who jostles us out of our parochialism, opens our minds to new vistas of **contemplation** and action, and challenges us to see, as in one of his favorite phrases, the "coincidence of opposites." He leads theology into the realm of the purely absolute and infinite, where in "inaccessible light" the beauty and splendor of the Lord's face can at last be approached "without veil."

When Nicholas died in Rome in August of 1464, he left to the library of the hospice approximately three hundred manuscripts devoted to theology, philosophy, civil and ecclesiastical law, science, history, and literature, as well as a large, personally edited portion of his sermons.

Nouwen, Henri J.M.

(1932-96) Priest, spiritual guide, author, and counselor, Nouwen insisted that the call of Jesus is a call to **conversion** of heart and deep healing, addressed not merely to saints but to the most ordinary people. He saw in the brokenness of humanity the wounded and glorified body of Jesus. No matter how lost one felt, he counseled, the way to one's true home could be found through God's unlimited and unconditional love.

Originally from the Netherlands, Nouwen spent most of his life in the United States, teaching at places like the Divinity Schools of Harvard and Yale, and taking time off to live in a Trappist abbey as well as to travel and live among the poor in Latin America. He found his final home in the L'Arche community called Daybreak in Toronto in a house devoted to the care of handicapped people. His conviction of its importance is clear: "Without some form of community, individual prayer cannot be born or developed. Communal and individual prayer belong together as two folded hands. Without community, individual prayer easily degenerates into egocentric and eccentric behavior, but without individual prayer, the prayer of the community quickly becomes a meaningless routine. Individual and community prayer cannot be separated without harm."

At L'Arche, Nouwen felt the full impact of what it meant to be a "wounded healer" for whom life itself becomes a preparation for death. He died of a heart attack in his native Holland almost to the day of his sixty-fourth birthday.

Obedience

Obedience, **poverty**, and **chastity** are the three evangelical counsels leading Christians in all walks of life to respond more fully and faithfully to God. The word "obedience" comes from the Latin *ob* and *audire*, meaning in English "to listen to" lawful authority, to God and the laws of God, and to the providential meaning of events in our life. By contrast, disobedience conveys the proud stance of one who isolates him or herself willfully from divine directives in daily life.

Whereas disobedience diminishes our freedom and entraps us in patterns of pride, anger, lust, and sloth, obedience is never closed or static. It affects our powers of listening, especially to the commandments of God. It impels us to make prudent choices, perhaps by asking what would Jesus do in this situation?

Christian obedience is always a sharing in the obedience of Jesus to his Father's will, as illumined in the concrete invitations, challenges, and appeals that make up our day-to-day life. We listen not alone but in and with the Church to what God asks of us as disciples of a wholly obedient Master. To honor his example, religious make a solemn vow of obedience according to their rule of life and in submission to their lawfully elected superiors.

To commit ourselves to a life of obedience may at times prove to be countercultural, but such is the risk we take when we pray with Jesus to the Father, "Not my will but yours be done" (Luke 22:42).

Origen

(c. 185-254) An Alexandrian Christian who witnessed his own father's martyrdom for the faith, Origen maintains his reputation as one of the most brilliant, if not controversial, theologians and masters of souls in the early Greek Church. An ordained priest, a specialist in philosophy, a teacher of catechesis, and a prolific author, Origen is largely responsible for the synthesis of platonic concepts and Christianity. So in love was he with God's Word that he wrote the first Christian *Commentary on the Song of Songs*, setting forth the pattern of the soul's **purgative**, **illuminative**, and **unitive** ascent to God through the most intimate of relationships with his Divine Word, Jesus Christ.

Origen's main contribution to Catholic teaching resides in his genius for systematic, ascetic, and mystical theology and biblical commentary, resulting in a method of interpretation that extended from an understanding of the letter of the text to its spiritual and symbolic meaning.

There was also a shadow side to Origen's brilliance. His father's death convinced him, as he wrote in *An Exhortation to Martyrdom*, that dying for Christ was the crown and summit of a true follower's life. His own desire to accompany his Divine Master to the death may explain the excesses of **asceticism** to which Origen was inclined, the least acceptable being self-castration. In the end, Origen got his wish. He had to endure savage torture for his beliefs, but nothing his persecutors inflicted upon him could induce him to deny his **faith**. He died as he lived—a man dedicated to modeling the threefold path of purgation, illumination, and union in perfect imitation of Christ crucified and glorified. He understood that the reward of endurance is "to enjoy with Christ Jesus the rest proper to blessedness, contemplating him, the Word wholly living."

One Step at a Time

One of the greatest evils of the day is the sense of futility. People say, "What can one person do? What is the sense of our small effort?" They cannot see that we can only lay one brick at a time, take one step at a time; we can be responsible only for the one action of the present moment. But we can beg for an increase of love in our hearts that will vitalize and transform these actions, and know that God will take them and multiply them, as Jesus multiplied the loaves and fishes.

–Dorothy Day

Padre Pio, Blessed

(1887-1968) Born in Pietrelcina, Italy, into a simple peasant family, the future saint was baptized Francesco Forgione. Following a peaceful and happy childhood, he entered the Capuchin novitiate of Morcone in 1903, taking the name of Fra (Brother) Pio (Pious). Ordained a priest in 1910 in the cathedral of Benevento, he then returned to his family for health reasons. In September of 1916, he entered the monastery of San Giovanni Rotondo in central Italy. Although at the time he believed his stay there would be only "temporary," in fact he remained there for the rest of his life.

On August 5, 1918, Padre Pio had a vision in which he felt himself pierced by a lance; subsequently he retained the signs of the lance-wound of the crucified Christ. A short while afterwards, on September 20, 1918, he also received the five wounds of our Lord's crucifixion in his hands and feet. They would remain with him until death. Despite the loss of blood each day, the wounds miraculously never closed nor festered, though the pain they caused the saint was palpable.

Complaints made against Padre Pio for his "unconventional" life resulted in his being suspended by the Congregation for the Doctrine of the Faith from all pastoral activities for a two-year period from 1931-1933, except for the private celebration of Mass. Padre Pio had his share of enemies, both supernatural (diabolical) and human, people who accused him of scandal in the world and even misunderstood his mission in the Church. But his life of heroic virtue and sanctity prevailed.

His whole mission on earth was to annihilate himself so that the source of his light, Jesus Christ, could shine through. "I am an instrument in divine hands," he said. "I am useful only when manipulated by the Divine Mover." He also ascribed the source of his strength to the **Blessed Virgin Mary**, calling the rosary his best defense against the demonic. He shared with people of all ages, cultures, social conditions, and professions his belief that "prayer is the best weapon I have; it is the key to God's heart. Speak to Jesus not only with your lips, but also with your heart." He had no doubt that "one searches for God in books, but will find him especially in prayer."

In May of 1955 Padre Pio established a well-equipped hospital at the San Giovanni Rotondo monastery, called the House for Relief of Suffering, to alleviate both the physical and spiritual misery he saw all around him. Padre Pio once said of his relation to the suffering of others: "I sense as my own your afflictions ... I will take on as my own all your sufferings ... and offer them for you as a holocaust to the Lord."

He made his final offering on September 23, 1968, when he passed away serenely. His tomb has since become a mecca for believers in search of inspiration and religious renewal. Pope John Paul II has said of Padre Pio: "The mysterious fruitfulness of his long life as a priest and as a religious son of **Saint Francis of Assisi** continues to operate and—we note—even with an unmistakable crescendo." On May 2, 1999, the Pope beatified him at Saint Peter's Basilica in Rome.

Peace

As one of the **fruits of the Holy Spirit**, peace, together with joy, is a sign that our will is one with God's will for us. To maintain this level of consonance may at times cause conflict between true disciples of Christ and others who would settle for peace at any price, even if this means the loss of their integrity. Jesus did not approve of such a compromising attitude. He himself warned the same disciples he had appointed ambassadors of peace, "Do not think that I have come to bring peace upon the earth. I have come to bring not peace but the sword" (Matthew 10:34). He even authorized the disciples to let their peace come upon a house, but if it was refused to "let your peace return to you" (Matthew 10:13).

Such cautions make it clear that the peace of which Jesus speaks is of a higher order. It may be hard to attain on earth, but we must try to live in peace, to go in peace, to bring peace with us. That is why we welcome the blessing bestowed upon us by the Church, citing the words of Saint Paul, "Grace to you and peace from God our Father and the Lord Jesus Christ" (1 Corinthians 1:3).

Entering into "the peace of God that surpasses all understanding" (Philippians 4:7) is a deeply formative experience, enabling us to radiate a peaceful presence to others and "to reconcile all things for [Christ]" (Colossians 1:20). Such Christ-formed peace is not a question of control but of living in union with the One who is the Ultimate Source of peaceful integration. Only if we see the divine unity behind every expression of diversity can we exercise the peacemaking capacity to reconcile opposing forces and quell their escalation.

Distrust and fear subside under the canopy of peace. One remains in rest and stillness before the Lord, in quiet and total surrender. We abandon our own will and follow the inner promptings of his Spirit. Such **obedience** is costly to our pride, but without it, no peace of soul is possible nor can we radiate this peace to others. This imperative of the apostle Paul gives us **hope** amidst the most bellicose circumstances: "May the God of peace himself make you perfectly holy and may you entirely, spirit, soul, and body, be preserved blameless for the coming of our Lord Jesus Christ" (1 Thessalonians 5:23).

Poverty of Spirit

In his Sermon on the Mount Jesus blesses the poor in spirit and assures them that the kingdom of heaven will be theirs (Matthew 5:3). This is because they find their **consolation** not in an abundance of worldly goods but in him. Jesus chooses to befriend the poor because their hearts are open enough to receive him. That is why, as the *Catechism* reminds us, love for the poor, indeed a preferential love, is part of the Church's constant tradition [2444].

While poverty is one of the evangelical counsels that characterize the vowed state of people called to the religious life [915], it is a virtue all followers of Christ must practice. Though he was rich, he became poor, "so that by his poverty [we] might become rich" (2 Corinthians 8:9). This way of dispossession involves more than diminishing our stock of excess worldly goods; it implies also that we detach ourselves from interior clutter, including our hunger for power, our need for worldly recognition, and our inclination to be possessive of both material and nonmaterial goods.

As Christians we are to imitate the poverty of Jesus illustrated in his hidden life in Nazareth, his powerlessness on the cross, his kenotic or self-emptying love. To show us what poverty of spirit really means Jesus did not cling to anything, not even to his equality with God (Philippians 2:6). He chose instead the condition of a servant, and so must we.

Our best model in this regard is the **Blessed Virgin Mary** in whose Magnificat we find the perfect prayer of the poor, for he who is mighty "has done great things for me, /and holy is his name ... /He has thrown down the rulers from their thrones /but lifted up the lowly. /The hungry he has filled with good things; /the rich he has sent away empty" (Luke 1:49-53). Like Mary, we, too, must become the poor instruments God uses to lead people closer to his kingdom and to the fullness of **peace** he promises to give us in Jesus.

Prayer of Intercession

Intercession is an essential vocation for all Christians. We are to be intercessors, asking God for **mercy** on each and every person in imitation of Christ. As we read in the Letter to the Hebrews, "Therefore, he is always able to save those who approach God through him, since he lives forever to make intercession for them" (Hebrews 7:25). Likewise, the Holy Spirit "intercedes for the holy ones according to God's will" (Romans 8:27).

It is important for us to realize that intercession originates in God, not in the intercessor. Because it is God who takes the initiative in intercessory prayer, this prayer is also **contemplative**. It presupposes that there is already a relationship of love between God and us, and between our neighbor in need and us. Intercession enables us to be with and for one another spiritually, even when we are far apart physically.

Recognition of our inadequacy and powerlessness does not imply that intercession is only a last resort. The apostle Paul reminds us that the intercession of Christians not only promotes intense fellowship; it also recognizes no boundaries. As he writes in his First Letter to Timothy: "I ask that supplications, prayers, petitions, and thanksgivings be offered for everyone, for kings and for all in authority, that we may lead a quiet and tranquil life in all **devotion** and dignity. This is good and pleasing to God our savior, who wills everyone to be saved and to come to knowledge of the truth" (1 Timothy 2:1-4).

Prayer of Petition

Though we are mere creatures and not our own masters, though we are sinners in need of redemption, we dare to plead for **mercy**, to **hope** against all hope, to groan, yearn, demand, beseech, and ask **forgiveness**. The prayer of forgiveness, is, according to the *Catechism*, the "first movement" of the prayer of petition [2631], a prayer best captured in the words of the Publican who said, "O God, be merciful to me a sinner" (Luke 18:13).

This disposition of trusting **humility** is the best posture for petitionary prayer. It mirrors Jesus' own sense of abandonment to the will of the Father and reminds us to never doubt that God will answer our prayers, even if the outcome of petition is contrary to our expectations. The prayer of petition must include our willingness to abide by God's reply, knowing that he always wills our good and understands the deeper reason for our petition in the first place.

A famous example of petitionary prayer can be found in the *Dialogue* of **Saint Catherine of Siena**. She organizes her thoughts in this book around four petitions: for herself, for the Church, for the whole world, and for God's providence over all, especially her spiritual father, Blessed Raymond of Capua. In answer to her petition for her own spiritual needs, God assures Catherine that he is entirely satisfied by her offering of herself to him in love, for with him love alone counts. As for the needs of the Church, he replies that he will reform her if only those who truly love him will offer themselves in prayer and penance for her renewal. In response to the saint's plea for the whole world, God answers with a promise to show mercy to all creatures by virtue of the prayers of the faithful. In regard to extending care to every single creature, and especially to her spiritual father, God says that she must encourage Raymond to work for the spiritual good of others and to make their good his sole concern. God granted Catherine's petitions; in praying them with her, they become our own.

Prayer of Presence

The prayer of presence is our way of emulating the boy Samuel, who said, "Speak, [Lord,] for your servant is listening" (1 Samuel 3:10). According to traditional wisdom, expressed by, among others, **Brother Lawrence of the Resurrection**, prayer is no more and no less than the practice of waiting upon and attending to God's presence at all times and in all places. It offers us the opportunity to slow down our busy pace and to feel refreshed in body, mind, and spirit. It fosters trustful openness to the wonders that surround us as well as relaxed in-touchness with daily life. No wonder the spiritual masters compare it to breathing. In the presence of the Divine Presence, the world is no longer merely the place in which we work; it is also the arena in which we **worship**.

To practice the prayer of presence is to recognize our personal need for God and to ready ourselves for any manifestation of his coming. We wait upon Divine Providence rather than pushing our plans. We ask the Spirit who prays in us to refine our sensitivity to the Father's will. At times this means praying in the darkness of not knowing. Our experience of God remains dim and obscure. We do believe he is there, we continue to love and adore him, though we do not feel his presence. Ours is a prayer of attentive desire—an aspiration of love reaching toward the Beloved as he is in himself. It is a prayer of openness to God as God, a mode of presence that remains as sturdy and true in **consolation** as in **desolation**. "For [when] we do not know how to pray as we ought ... the Spirit itself intercedes with inexpressible groanings" (Romans 8:26-27).

Prayer of the Heart

The heart's devoted turning to God, sustained by reading and reflection, is an exercise in simplicity that renders us open, receptive, and abandoned to the mystery, majesty, and **mercy** of God. It is comparable to breathing, to beholding the wonder of things with the eyes of a child, to believing in the Most High, who lovingly holds us in the palm of a mighty yet tender hand. This sort of prayer takes many forms: a longing for sweetness, a cry for mercy, a song of joy, a wordless exchange of love between friends, an awareness of affinity, or a gasp of gratitude when the ordinary suddenly becomes extraordinary. It is the soaring of the human spirit to meet and be one with the Spirit of God. It is heart calling to Heart, the alone with the Alone, the finite before the Infinite, the temporal at home with the Eternal.

To pray in this way is to love God with our whole heart, soul, mind, and strength; it is to become the fully alive persons the Beloved intends us to be. According to the tradition of the Christian East, when such an ordering of the heart occurs, everything in our head passes into our heart. This is "the union of the mind with the heart" or "the prayer of the mind in the heart."

Prompted by Pure Love

When our hearts are truly abandoned we embrace every possible kind of spirituality, for our whole being gives itself up to God's will, and this act of surrender, prompted by pure love, means that we involve ourselves in all that pleases him.

–Jean-Pierre de Caussade

A kind of mental light illumines our entire inner being. No matter what we do or say or think, all is done with full consciousness and attention. By this light, we can more clearly see what in us conforms to Christ and what does not. With heart, mind, and will, we are set to obey his Word.

Our prayer at such times may be no more than a peaceful telling of our love, an offering of adoration and dedication, a felt sorrow for sin. At moments of deepest intimacy, we may be united with God in total **silence**, in a bond of lasting communion. However excellent our channels of human communication may be, there are times when all dialogue ceases save conversation with Christ. He becomes our dearest companion in labor and leisure as we make room within our hearts for his holy revelations.

Pseudo-Dionysius

(c. 500) This enigmatic yet profoundly influential spiritual figure, possibly a Syrian monk of the sixth century, wrote under the pseudonym of Dionysius the Aeropagite, whom the apostle Paul converted. His writings reveal a distinct preference for the *via negativa* or "negative way theology" that stresses the utter inability of the human mind to penetrate the impenetrable abyss of the mystery of God.

In his seminal book *The Mystical Theology*, he introduces the threefold path of **purgation, illumination**, and **union** that has become classical in the West. The Dionysian tradition discriminates between beginners, proficients, and the perfect and mentions three types of Christians: (1) those introduced to or approaching **contemplation,** whose main concern is the practice of virtue (*praxis*); (2) those in the middle way to whom contemplation (*theoria*) and the suppressions of passions (*apatheia*) are particularly suitable; and finally (3) the perfect, to whom God reveals in an experiential way knowledge of himself (*theologia*). These various stages are understood to interpenetrate one another. They demarcate movements in the human soul responsive to divine transformation.

Many mystics after Pseudo-Dionysius expounded on this tradition, notably the anonymous author of ***The Cloud of Unknowing*** and **Saint John of the Cross**, both of whom mention "Denys" by name. By the sixth century, his writings were already known and commented upon by **Saint Maximus the Confessor**. From the eleventh century onward, many more commentaries appeared after being translated into Latin, notably one by **Saint Thomas Aquinas** on *The Divine Names.*

Dionysius himself believed that God is above all names. He is a Being beyond being itself, residing in the dark reality of the super-essential nature of the Godhead that always and forever defies definition. Dionysius stresses the impotence of every human attempt to penetrate the veil that stands between God and us. God draws us through purification to deification. We must bow in **humility** before his allness and acknowledge our nothingness. In this **prayer of petition,** he summarizes his longing to be led by the mystery of the **Blessed Trinity** to new depths of knowing in unknowing:

> Trinity!! Higher than any being,
> any divinity, any goodness!
> Guide of Christians
> in the wisdom of heaven!
> Lead us up beyond unknowing and
> light,
> up to the farthest, highest peak
> of mystic scripture,
> where the mysteries of God's Word

lie simple, absolute and unchangeable
in the brilliant darkness of a hidden silence.
Amid the deepest shadow
they pour overwhelming light
on what is most manifest.
Amid the whole unsensed and unseen
they completely fill our sightless minds
with treasures beyond all beauty.

Purgative Way (Purgation)
The Holy Spirit uses the early or initial periods of our unfolding in Christ to awaken us to God's love and the outpouring of grace in our here-and-now existence. These inspirations and aspirations compel us to seek God with a more ardent love, but they also remind us of the stark contrast between his will and our willfulness, his goodness and our stubborn resistance. This awakening is accompanied by the graces of purification.

Saint John of the Cross compares this point on our journey to early evening or twilight. It marks our departure from a former way of life, shadowed by selfish sensuality, to the dawning of a new life in Christ. The question is: Are we willing to carry the cross that detaches us from worldly pleasures, powers, and possessions as ultimate? We sense that these must undergo mortification or dying to self if we are to be reborn in Christ. Saint John calls these purgations the nights of sense and spirit. He observes with great accuracy in his book, *The Dark Night*, "that all the imperfections and disorders of the sensory part are rooted in the spirit and from it receive their strength. All good and evil habits reside in the spirit and until these are purged the senses cannot be completely purified of their rebellions and vices."

Cleansed by grace are the gross pollutants that blind us to the truth of our absolute dependence on God. Stripped away, at times in a flood of sorrowful tears, is our sinful tendency to put self before God. As we begin to mortify these inordinate attachments to any person, event, or thing as more important than God, grace may draw us still deeper into the night, where the only means of ascent is **faith**. Still more secret and intimate self-communications of God await us in the **illuminative** and **unitive ways**, but for now we need the nights of purgation to catapult us from the surface of life to its depths with the Crucified Christ at our side.

Only the cleansing powers of spiritual purgation can restore the dull veneer left on our life by the parasites of self-centeredness and prepare us to enter the land of union and likeness to

God. Paradoxical as it may seem, purgation is the key to spiritual liberation. God's way with us seems to demand profound **detachment** from what we know we must leave behind for the sake of finding it again as hidden in the mystery of God's eternal, providential care. In short, by withdrawing from attachments to lesser goods in the purgative way, we come to appreciate the highest good, the God of Love, to whom they point.

Purity of Heart

This graced disposition flourishes in souls whose intellects and wills aim at one thing only: a life of holiness. Given to us as the fruit of purification of heart is the privilege of beholding God in the Beatific Vision. As the Beatitude proclaims, "Blessed are the clean of heart, /for they shall see God" (Matthew 5:8). Since the heart is "the seat of moral personality" [2517], the purer it is, the better we can see according to God's commands and ways. The *Catechism* also points out how purity of heart, together with purity of intention and modesty, cleanse the social climate in which we live [2525]. Living in respectful presence to persons enables us to "perceive the human body—ours and our neighbor's—as a temple of the Holy Spirit, a manifestation of divine beauty" [2519].

It is the Lord himself who invites us to purity of heart, with all its demands, and the same Lord who promises that we shall see the Absolute Beauty, the Triune God, who is the source of all goodness and the object of our longing. Many attitudes prepare us for this transformation, but only the redemptive love of Jesus can release our hearts from temptations to self-indulgence. Thus freed, we can love God with our whole being and others in him. In short, all is of God and for God. We rest in the shadow of his protection and favor.

This love is an earthly semblance of that ineffable **peace** and joy we shall experience in the life to come. In the common ways of home or business, in the drabness of passing days, in moments of pleasure and pain, we strive to see the Lord's face where others may see only frustration and despair. Jesus saw the face of the Father in all of creation. He beheld and called forth the inmost divine form of each disciple. This divinized seeing is the Lord's gift to us. Through it, he embraces the whole world and each unique person, comprehending what we need before we ask. Our entire life is mirrored in his sight. God is one with us, and in our hearts we have become one with him as we pray with the psalmist:

A clean heart create for me, O God,
and a steadfast spirit renew within me.
Cast me not out from your presence,
and your holy spirit take not from me.
Give me back the joy of your salvation,
and a willing spirit sustain in me.

Psalm 51:12-14

> ### *Queen Humility*
>
> There's no queen like humility
> for making the King surrender.
> Humility drew the King from
> heaven to the womb of the
> Virgin, and with it, by one hair
> we will draw him to our souls.
>
> –*Saint Teresa of Avila*

Quietism

This false form of **mysticism** arose in the seventeenth century under the impetus, among others, of Madame Guyon and Miguel de Molinos. They espoused a doctrine that once one makes an act of submission to God, one should engage in no further attempt to acquire virtue or to resist temptation. In other words, the quietist wittingly or unwittingly disengages mysticism from its ascetic foundations and makes the experience of inner quieting an end in itself.

This heresy was a grave departure from the authentic tradition of prayer associated with inner calm and quiet presence to the Lord that extends from the writings of Eastern Church Fathers like **Evagrius Ponticus** to classical masters of the Western Church like **Saint Teresa of Avila**. Letting go of inordinate attachments and of hungering for spiritual **consolations** help one to mature in the life of prayer. The inner quiet associated with spiritual equilibrium was called by **Saint Ignatius of Loyola** and **Saint Francis de Sales** "holy indifference." They recommend that especially during periods of **aridity** one needs to resign oneself to God's will as revealed in the present circumstances of one's life and in the teachings and traditions of the Church.

Abandonment to Divine Providence means not only receptive openness to what comes about in life through the allowing **will of God** but also active acceptance of it in full trust and love. The trouble comes when quieting one's illusions of control or calming one's fears turns into a wholly passive state indifferent to Church laws and precepts. One's claim to total abandonment and an absolutely disinterested love of God denies the need for any human effort at all.

Quietism discourages self-reflection, striving for virtue, repelling temptations, or engaging in any inner activity whatsoever. This heresy goes so far as to suggest that the state of perfect passivity may be consonant with objectively sinful behavior. Quietism, understood as purely passive inwardness, is in no way authentically Christian nor are the aberrations it spawns, among others, apathetic indifference toward good and evil, resignation to one's fate, lack of regret for one's past sins, and aloofness to the plight of the poor.

The Church condemned quietism in 1675. However, its condemnation must not be mistaken as a negation of mysticism as such but as a proper warning of how disconnected the best intentions can be from an authentic approach to the interior life that balances **contemplation** and action, quiet adoration and creative service.

> ### *Restoring Grace*
>
> Whoever wishes to ascend to God must first avoid sin, which deforms our nature, then exercise his natural powers ... by praying, to receive restoring grace; by a good life, to receive purifying justice; by meditating, to receive illuminating knowledge; and by contemplating, to receive perfecting wisdom.
>
> *–Saint Bonaventure*

Richard of Saint Victor

(d. 1173) The most mystical member of the Abbey of Saint Victor in Paris, Richard's treatises exerted a profound influence on medieval and modern mysticism. He entered the abbey to study under the famous scholastic theologian and philosopher Hugh of Saint Victor. Richard became superior in 1159 and prior in 1162.

The Victorines were erudite in Holy Scripture and the Latin Fathers and showed much interest in the link between theology and **mysticism.** Richard's thinking was not dry and abstract but biblical and experiential. The Bible was the basis of his theological thought. In this regard, he enjoys an affinity with **Saint Augustine, Saint Anselm of Canterbury**, and **Saint Bernard of Clairvaux**, all of whom focused on a loving **contemplation** of God rather than on a strict scholastic approach.

For Richard, the act of contemplation is a function of **faith** in search of insight and unification with God. He held that seekers must pursue secular learning as well as study divine revelation, but that in all things faith in God's guidance must prevail. He describes the six stages of contemplation, from sense perception or the simple awareness of things, to worship or a deeper grasp of the epiphanic design of creation, to an intuition of the inner reality of the soul.

At the heights of contemplation, one apprehends truth beyond reason so as to share in a kind of divine ecstasy, leading to that abiding **peace** wherein one is united through grace with God. To each of these stages there corresponds a spiritualization of knowledge and a higher form of love, starting with loving our neighbor as we love ourselves, and proceeding to utter oneness with God.

Employing in his mystical works an extensive symbolism reminiscent of the

Alexandrian School, Richard made the School of Saint Victor famous throughout the twelfth and into the thirteenth century. His *Benjamin Major* and *Benjamin Minor* became standard manuals on the practice of mystical spirituality in medieval times. Richard's mystical theology continued to influence the Church through the writings of **Saint Bonaventure** and the Franciscan School.

Rolle, Richard

(c. 1300-1349) Rolle is first in the line of mystics who blessed the Church in England in the fourteenth century. Much to his parents' dismay, he grew disillusioned with his studies at the University of Oxford. He found especially distasteful the proclivity toward endless theological disputation. He left there without a degree to establish himself as a hermit on a private estate. Later he moved to other hermitages and led a rather nomadic existence while offering occasional spiritual direction to a group of nuns at Hampole in South Yorkshire.

In his life and writings Rolle reveals an ardent love for God and a rapturous attraction to the sweet intimacy of encounter with his Son, Jesus Christ. In exalting the life of **solitude** and **contemplation**, he urged strict and at times extreme self-control. He does show in his meditations on Holy Scripture that spiritual progress consists mainly in developing one's love of God, a love consummated in mystical union, not in the excesses of mortification. His method of instruction includes the ascetic dimension, but it consists ultimately of concentrating one's affections on the person of Jesus Christ, which results in an experience of intense joy.

Rolle was fond of calling attention to the "mirth of God" side by side with the mundane folly of choosing worldliness over the ways of **poverty**, **chastity**, and **obedience**. God granted him, as he had **Saint Francis of Assisi**, the ability to see signs of the sacred everywhere—in nature, in the poor, in the souls he served as a spiritual director, and even in those who caused him to carry the cross of unjust critique. Through it all, his love for the Holy Name of Jesus and for the Bible enabled him to triumph over hardships and to arouse in others the fire of love that consumed his own heart and raised it to heaven.

Ruysbroeck, Blessed John

(1293-1381) A central figure among the Flemish mystics, Ruysbroeck was born in Brabant in an era marked by such cataclysmic events as the Hundred Years' War, the Black Death, numerous peasant uprisings, and enough turmoil to be designated as the "age of adversity." The Church fared no better than the social order, wracked as it was by the decline of the mendicant orders, the split in the papacy between Rome and Avignon, and the rise of the Free Spirits, a heresy that strove to demean the Church and its sacramental spirituality in favor of a subjectivistic, even pantheistic, experience of God.

Yet in the midst of such catastrophes there arose in the Church a number of great mystics, who, in addition to Ruysbroeck, included **Saint Catherine of Siena** in Italy, **John Tauler** in Germany, and **Julian of Norwich** in England, to name only a few.

Despite his lack of formal education, Ruysbroeck was a man of great intellectual energy, as at home in the active life as in the contemplative. To steer a steady course through the chaos surrounding him, he founded with his uncle and fellow priest a contemplative community in the countryside. There he followed his own bent toward the interior life. Stripping away all preconceived concepts of God, he sought an avenue to that "superessential" unity at the heart of our being.

Ruysbroeck's four great works reflect his understanding of the spiritual life as a graduated procession from spiritual courtship and espousal to spiritual marriage or deification. In every soul, Ruysbroeck taught, there dwells as its root and essence the eternal image of God. This image is Trinitarian, for we humans are a "created Trinity." That is why Ruysbroeck traces in *The Spiritual Espousals* the journey of the soul from the active, to the interior, to the contemplative life.

In another book of his, *The Sparkling Stone,* he names the four things necessary for a perfect life: to be zealous and good, interiorly fervent and spiritual, lifted up to the contemplation of God, and outreaching to all without discrimination of any. In this progression from contemplation to action, one grows through an increase in grace to such Christlikeness that one becomes, as his third book indicates, *A Mirror of Eternal Blessedness.* For the soul who enjoys God in this state, there is, according to Ruysbroeck, "nothing but oneness" between the eternal blessedness of God and his chosen ones. In his final work, *The Little Book of Clarification,* he tries to explain the nature of union with the Trinity or our ascent to "eternal beatitude" in which we are "raised above ourselves to God and become one spirit with God in love."

S

Seton, Saint Elizabeth Ann

(1774-1821) A native of New York City, Elizabeth was the daughter of Richard Bayley, an esteemed medical doctor and professor, and Catherine Charlton, daughter of an Episcopal rector. Elizabeth grew up in an atmosphere of wealth and privilege, though, as was the custom in those days, she lived apart from her family, and none too happily, while attending school. When she was twenty years old, she married William Seton, a shipping merchant, and eventually became the mother of five children. They lived in Manhattan.

Elizabeth enjoyed good times, characterized by her **spiritual reading**, religious fervor, and work with the poor, but also many tribulations including family deaths, sicknesses, and a decline in her husband's business to the point of bankruptcy. Through all these years Elizabeth practiced faithfully the Episcopalian religion of her youth. To help restore William's failing health, the Setons went on a trip to Italy from which William would never return. He died in 1803, leaving her a widow at the age of twenty-nine, having been married just eight years.

It was in Italy under the influence of friends that Elizabeth was introduced to and felt an attraction for the Catholic **faith**. She returned home, continued to pray about her life call, and finally, in March of 1805, converted to Catholicism, even though this meant considerable alienation from friends and family members.

Elizabeth found it hard to earn a living because of the animosity she encountered. When she was offered the chance in 1806 to conduct a school for girls in Baltimore, she did so with joy. She moved to Emmitsburg, Maryland, a few years later. There, together with several companions, she adopted a modified rule of the Daughters of Charity of **Saint Vincent de Paul** and thus became the foundress of the first American religious order, the Sisters of Charity.

In addition to caring for and educating her own children, Elizabeth laid the cornerstone of the parochial school system in the United States. She trained teachers and prepared textbooks. She translated books from French to English, wrote spiritual reflections, visited the poor and the sick, established several orphanages, and developed a deep love for the **Eucharist**. Her motto of life could be summarized in one sentence of hers: "We may be sure that our Savior offers himself *for each one* of us every time *we* offer our whole soul and body there with him." Simply put, "to love him with the whole heart is all."

In 1975, Elizabeth became the first American woman to be canonized a saint. The national shrine that houses her remains is in Emmitsburg, Maryland, in the Chapel of Saint Joseph's Provincial House of the Sisters of Charity.

Silence

Inner silence is the disposition that most readies us to hear the Word of God with the ears of our heart. Considering the noise and speed of modern life, it is necessary to create, at least inwardly if not outwardly, a climate of quiet and stillness.

Being in silence enables us to create an inner space in which to encounter God on a more profound level. Our exchange is, in a sense, beyond words. In that silent center, where the Holy Spirit prays in our hearts, we transcend our own limitations. Stilled, like a child on its mother's lap, we are with God and God is with us. We are wordlessly present to one another, yet a world of communication transpires between us. Because language cramps this reality, we fall silent. Words signifying human mastery dissolve as we listen to God's song. During such gratuitous moments, we are in tune with a silent treasure, God's presence in the core of our being.

Lacking silence, we are likely to process information in piecemeal fashion. Our mind starts to race, distractions dart in and out, and before long we lose our train of thought. We can hardly hold on to one idea before another rushes in. A common problem, related to why we may seek to escape silence, is the discovery that it evokes from within a bedlam of doubts, guilt feelings, and often disquieting fears. If we can let go of these **distractions in prayer** and remain silent, we may experience a gradual waning of inner noise. Silence becomes like a creative space in which we regain our spiritual perspective. In silence the scattered pieces of our life fall into place, and we see again where we are going.

This deep silence warms our hearts, and reminds us that in the midst of the ups and downs of daily life we stand on the firm ground of God's unchanging love. He assures us of this love not in flashes of lightning or furious thunder but in soft, gentle breezes (1 Kings 19:13). We wait upon God in these gifted moments as God waits upon us.

Silence of this depth touches every sphere of our existence. It brings to the body the grace of relaxation, to the mind the benefit of increased attention. It makes possible thoughtful speech and leads to more effective action. Most of all, silence enables us to be centered in God.

Solitude

Solitude means having a center within ourselves where we can be alone and at the same time at one with our Lord. Since most of us do not have an opportunity to enjoy lengthy experiences of outer **silence** and solitude, we have to learn to find the essence of these experiences within.

The opportunity to find outer solitude is not as prevalent in the lives of Christians in the world as it is for cloistered contemplatives, and yet all of us can strive to preserve at least inner solitude. We can adopt this attitude anywhere, though doing so requires discipline and resolve.

The more mindful we are that God is appealing to us in persons, events, and things, the more it becomes "second nature" to step aside from the workaday world and its pressures and to find some place and time to be alone with God. We can try wherever we are—in a busy bus depot or in the midst of a public meeting—to quiet ourselves inwardly so that we can listen to God's voice. We can put to rest agitation, tension, and needless worry. Our attention shifts from these concerns to God. Legitimate cares continue to call for action, but they no longer consume us. We allow ourselves, if only for a brief while, to be alone with the Alone.

Such an approach may have the side benefit of preventing impulsive, unwise decisions. By relaxing in solitude, we are more likely to discover the best course of action. This disposition becomes the bridge to true communion and empathic communication. Christ responded to the needs of the crowds who followed him, but only after he went off to a lonely place to pray and obey the voice of the Father (Mark 1:35). Like the Lord, we, too, must give witness to a joyful spirituality that progresses through solitude to an increasing depth of intimacy with and ministry to other people.

Spiritual Childhood

When the disciples argued among themselves as to who was the greatest in God's eyes, Jesus called a child to himself. Rebuking them for their bickering, he said, "Unless you turn and become like children, you will not enter the kingdom of heaven" (Matthew 18:3).

In this passage, Jesus is not counseling his disciples to be childish. He invites them as adults to enter a kind of second childhood where wisdom replaces naiveté and confidence in God overrides the illusion of control.

Many little ones pave the highway of sanctity in the Catholic Church, and none more so than the young woman who wrote specifically of this way in her *Story of a Soul*, **Saint Thérèse of Lisieux**. She tells us that Jesus showed her that the only path that leads to the heart of love is that of complete abandonment, like a baby who sleeps without fear in her father's arms.

It was the "little soul" of Saint Thérèse that attracted God's greatness and enabled him to turn her nothingness into living fire. In the menial tasks of everyday life in the convent—doing laundry, setting tables, caring for the infirm—she realized her "little way." Each duty became an act of love for her "*Abba*." Saint Thérèse's example of spiritual childhood can inspire us to move from a fragmented to a simple life centered in the love-will of Jesus for the Father.

A sure sign of spiritual childhood is the disposition of **abandonment to Divine Providence** in the here-and-now circumstances of daily life. We find that our deepest intention is to love God as perfectly as possible, whatever sacrifices this may entail. This love requires the firm commitment to please the Beloved in all things and to unite our will wholly with the **will of God**. The result is spiritual simplicity, a being at one with our Lord in all that we think, will, and do.

Only the Lamb of God can give this gift of simplicity to us. Christ is the perfect child of the Father, and we are to imitate him in all things, believing that he hides himself in our heart and works in us in a mysterious manner, inspiring us through his Spirit to make our life an embodiment of his eternal, infinite love of souls.

Spiritual Direction

This art and discipline encompasses three interrelated aspects, defined by **Adrian van Kaam** as private or one-on-one direction, direction-in-common, and spiritual self-direction.

The first way is especially necessary at crisis moments in one's faith journey or when one is led by grace to higher planes of prayer and **contemplation**. To offer private direction in these delicate matters, one has to be, in the words of **Saint Teresa of Avila**, wise, learned, and experienced. Wise directors embody the common wisdom of the Church. Their study of Scripture and the masters enables them to understand the life of the spirit also in the light of ascetic and mystical theology. They are experienced enough to avoid building dependent relations in the name of spiritual direction. They also know when to refer someone to other experts in counseling, psychiatry, or psychotherapy for the help they need.

The way of direction-in-common is the most universal form of guidance offered by the Church. It imitates Christ's own way of teaching gatherings of believers and unbelievers. What Jesus said made sense to many of them both personally and communally. The Word of God became the guiding light of their life. Direction-in-common invites us to remain open to divine directives emanating from such reliable sources as spiritual conferences, homilies, and lectures, from shared **spiritual reading** groups, prayer, and Bible study sessions. Such occasions deepen and strengthen our commitment to Christ; they teach us how to grow in intimacy with God through the common ways of **spiritual formation**. We learn to hear and heed the appeals, invitations, and challenges of Spirit-inspired self-direction in the situations of everyday life. For example, the Holy Spirit can and often does use a text read formatively as a means to communicate a message that can be life-transforming.

Spiritual self-direction makes us more receptive to the forming, reforming, and transforming presence and action of the **Blessed Trinity**. Knowing that we stand under the loving gaze of God makes us less prone to push ourselves beyond the pace of grace. We learn instead to respond to grace and to take responsibility for our decisions and actions. Most of all we strive over a lifetime of spiritual self-direction to be faithful to our unique-communal call and vocation. Another person can facilitate our efforts, but only God can lead us to full and loving knowledge of his will for our lives.

Spiritual Formation

Our Christian tradition offers to all believers three basic paths to spiritual awakening. These are liturgy, word, and sacrament, also designated the common ways of spiritual formation. These are practiced in general in the faith community while helping each individual to pursue his or her personal call to spiritual deepening and a life devoted to **meditation**, prayer, love, and service in Christ's name:

1) *Liturgy.* Many faith groupings in Christianity—for example, the Roman Catholic, Orthodox, Episcopalian and Lutheran—teach the fundamental importance and centrality of liturgy, ritual, and symbol in the worship experience. Our coming before God in reverence and adoration depends in great measure on the overall quality of the spiritual life of presiders and participants alike.

2) *Word.* The people of God are led to a fuller awareness of their **faith** through hearing and reading the Word

of God in Scripture and in the texts of our tradition, some of which are identified as the **classics of Christian spirituality**. The Word of God is compared to a seed which is sown in a field; those who hear this Word with faith become part of the flock Christ came to call and redeem (cf. Matthew 13:1-9). They receive, through the Word, entrance to God's reign. Then, by its own power, the seed sprouts and grows until harvest time.

Catholic teaching holds that Christ himself is present in his Word since it is he himself who speaks when the Holy Scriptures are read in the Church. For the Word of God to bear solid fruit in daily life, it must be heard with the inner ears of the heart. If one is to "go into the whole world and proclaim the Gospel to every creature" (Mark 16:15), the Word has to be the center of one's thoughts, decisions, and actions.

3) *Sacrament.* Our tradition teaches that it is only through the "sacramental economy," through worthy reception of the sacraments, that what is proclaimed in the Word of God and celebrated liturgically is fulfilled. Availing oneself frequently of the sacraments is a common means toward Christian perfection and the realization of the universal **call to holiness**. Together with **Baptism** and **Confirmation**, worthy reception of the Body and Blood of Christ is the principal means of formation of the people of God and of their salvation.

Spiritual Friendship

According to the *Catechism,* chaste friendship, whether between persons of the same or opposite sex, is a great good that "leads to spiritual communion" [2347]. Soul-friends make sacrifices for one another. They obey the laws of the Lord governing everything from adoration to sexual abstinence. They respect confidentiality at a level of heart-to-heart intimacy that unites them to one another in God.

Faith in the Lord and commitment to his will is the basis of every soul-friendship. Our oneness in God makes it possible for us to share prayer, to confess our secret hopes and dreams, to endure hardships, and celebrate joys. It enables us not only to befriend one another but to offer inclusive love to all who come our way.

Just as the Father wills our total good, so we will the entire good of the friends he sends to us. That being so, spiritual friendship is neither possessive nor manipulative; rather it is an affinity rooted in appreciation and **compassion**.

Saint Aelred of Rievaulx, who wrote a classic on *spiritual friendship*, warns against an exclusivity that binds people together emotionally but at the expense of eroding their **charity**. Aelred saw the true marks of friendship as frankness and not flattery, generosity and not gain, patience in correction, and constancy in affection. In this way, from being a friend to others, we become friends of God.

Saint John of the Cross cautions souls under his direction to foster equal love (inclusivity) and equal forgetfulness (**detachment**). Lacking this capacity for befriending others, we may be caught in the barbed wire of resentment, envy, and jealousy. Equal love, as Saint Paul teaches in 1 Corinthians 13:4-13, is patient and kind; it is never boastful or conceited, rude or selfish, and it does not come to an end as fickle romantic love is wont to do. Where there is strife, soul-friends seek avenues of reconciliation. When tempers flare and impatience prevails, they ask God for the grace to make a new start.

In *The Way of Perfection,* **Saint Teresa of Avila** counseled her sisters to avoid gossip and those rash judgments that can destroy community life. Instead, the saint asked her sisters to befriend one another by commending to God anyone at fault and, when observing a fault, striving to practice the opposite virtue. It is often in such times of crisis that friends discover their shared vulnerability and their need to care for one another as God cares for them. Then they can go out and bear fruit that will last (John 15:8), knowing that "a true friend is more loyal than a brother" (Proverbs 18:24).

Spiritual Reading as Art

The practice of spiritual reading as an art nourishes the life of the spirit and leads us to various resources in the literature of spirituality that help us to focus on such fundamental themes of spiritual deepening as **silence, humility, compassion**, and **obedience**.

The Bible is the primary and most basic text for spiritual reading. Background reading (doctrinal, exegetical, historical) can be done at a time other than that set aside for this exercise. Even such informational reading can become spiritual to a degree because this kind of study centers our attention on the text at hand and draws us to meditation on its meaning for us. Like good artists, we strive to eliminate all utilitarian and ulterior motives so as to be solely intent on listening to the Word of God as it manifests itself through the reading.

In short, spiritual reading is an art requiring the reader to develop attitudes more or less different from those required for informational reading. These two types of reading are complementary, but we have to develop a kind of "sixth sense" by which we know when to switch from level to level—when, so to speak, to take off our "student hat" and put on our "disciple hat." We can use the same text on one occasion for study and on another for spiritual reading. The more we are able to sense interiorly when the shift has to be made, the more capable we will become as spiritual readers.

During spiritual reading time, we seek to receive the message of the Master in whatever degree we are capable of opening up to it. What is the Holy Spirit offering in the limited passage we are reading? Our attitude as spiritual readers is more docile and receptive, less dialectical and comparative.

Where informational reading tends to be rather dissective (taking pieces of spiritual knowledge from here and there to increase erudition), spiritual reading is more dynamic (adroit at making connections between what we are reading and our life here and now).

The purpose of spiritual reading is not to fully understand the text in that mode of mastery we need when, for instance, we take a Scripture course, but to derive from it spiritual inspiration and nourishment. Peacefully and quietly, we read the text with an openness of mind and heart, seeking in it what speaks meaningfully to us in our present situation. We derive from reading not just spiritual erudition but a deepening of our personal relation to God. Whereas informational reading may nourish one part of us—our analytical intelligence—spiritual reading sustains the deepest part, that inner spirit where God dwells and desires to permeate our whole life.

Spiritual Reading as Discipline

Spiritual reading is not only an art; it is also a discipline requiring certain conditions to facilitate this practice and to remove obstacles to the action of grace. For example, we have to set a time for regular reading and adhere to it as much as possible. A commonly agreed upon length is every day for at least twenty minutes.

Time is at a premium for us all. However, if growth in the spiritual life becomes our main priority, as it should be, we will want to make time for it. Setting the right time, choosing when to do spiritual reading, and sticking to it are important phases of this discipline. Each of us has a unique pace of spiritual progress that must be in tune with the given organic rhythms of our body. If we keep that correlation in mind, we are likely to choose an alert time for our devotional practices rather than letting them go until the end of the day or pushing them off until everything else gets done.

In addition to finding time for spiritual reading, it is also necessary to set aside a quiet space or place where we will not be disturbed and where we can be fully present to the text at hand. Whether we know it or not on the conscious level, we are influenced by the space we inhabit. When walking into a gothic cathedral, the space does something to us that is different from what happens when we go to the bus depot. The space of the cafeteria at lunchtime affects us differently than when we go to an exquisite restaurant for an elegant dinner. That is why every spiritual practice may become more fruitful if we take into account our surroundings. It is wiser, therefore, to do spiritual reading in our own room, in the chapel, or in a familiar setting than trying to get it done on the bus going to work or while eating a quick lunch.

The very act of following our set time and sitting or standing in our favorite place with a well-chosen text in hand already begins to slow us down. Even before the period of reading begins, we have been put in that more dwelling, docile, receptive mood that prepares us in heart and mind to receive God's message. Some days it will be easier to do this than others, but distractions and lack of discipline ought not to upset us unduly. It is amazing how fast the "honeymoon period" is over for any devotional practice. The excitement of newness lasts only a short while.

When routine and boredom tempt us to put off the practice, we do it anyway thanks to the effects of regular repetition. Days will dawn when, in spite of our willingness and openness, reading means little or nothing to us. Now is not the time to be discouraged. It is exactly the day-after-dayness of religious practice that matters. What counts for God is that we remain faithful to our reading, even though we feel inwardly arid. By doing our formative reading day after day, we show God our good will and open our hearts to the grace of spiritual deepening.

Surrender to God

Father,
I surrender myself into your hands;
do with me what you will.
Whatever you may do, I thank you:
I am ready to accept everything.

As long as your will is done in me
and in all your creatures.
I wish no more than this, O Lord.

Into your hands I commend my soul:
I give it to you
with all the love of my heart,
for I love you, Lord,
and I need to give myself,
to yield myself to you without reserve
and with boundless confidence,
for you are my Father.

–Charles de Foucauld

Stein, Edith

See **Saint Teresa Benedicta of the Cross.**

Suso, Blessed Henry

(c. 1295-1366) Having grown up near Lake Constance on the border between Germany and Switzerland, Suso entered the Dominican friary at an early age. While in the monastery, he underwent a conversion experience and became a devoted follower of his fellow Dominican **Meister Eckhart,** whose cause he defended. He had to learn over the course of time that the road to the inner life was not paved by harsh physical chastisement, scrupulosity, or morbid **asceticism**, but by the practice of knowing and loving God in his suffering humanity.

Destined to become one of the chief representatives of German **mysticism,** Suso shared with laity and fellow religious his gifts for preaching, **spiritual direction**, and writing. In his first work, *The Little Book of Truth* (c. 1327), he extols the value of submission to God and self-denial for his sake. He also wrote *The Little Book of Eternal Wisdom,* an autobiography comparable to **Saint Augustine's** *Confessions* and a book almost as popular as *The Imitation of Christ* by **Thomas à Kempis.**

One distinctive feature of Suso's spirituality is the conviction he holds that mysticism, far from being a matter of powerful feelings, aims for a vision without images, for immersion in the Godhead and intimacy with Christ's humanity. Though Suso's writings are richly lyric and poetic, with an appeal to popular piety, he also has the ability to fuse theological reflection and everyday formation. His **devotion** to the divine name of Jesus and his disposition of perfect **detachment** so as "to receive everything as from God" are other marks of his spirituality. As he once wrote, "Some people come and talk on and on about lofty perfection and have never taken the first step. They do not know how to abandon themselves the least little bit."

Abandonment to Divine Providence was the one discipline above any other that Suso prayed to attain. His veneration for the **Blessed Virgin Mary** is a noticeable feature of his life and work, as is his emphasis on total self-renunciation as the royal road to mystical union. He urges us to meditate on the Passion of Christ and to turn to Mary, who stands with us at the foot of our own crosses as our protectress and intercessor.

Suso spent the last years of his life as a wandering preacher and spiritual director of mainly the Dominican nuns and the Friends of God in Switzerland. He endured physical hardship and persecution by people who questioned his mission, but through it all he remained espoused to Lady Wisdom, in whom all his longings found fulfillment.

Symeon the New Theologian

(c. 945-1022) A great mystic of Eastern Christianity, Symeon left the countryside when he was a young man to come to Constantinople to study. There, under the guidance of God, he found his monastic vocation in 977. Shortly thereafter, inspired by the intensity of his prayer life, his rigorous **asceticism**, and his outstanding gifts for **spiritual direction** and conventual discipline, his brothers elected him abbot.

Symeon is noted in the Orthodox tradition for his **devotion** to the Holy Spirit and his belief that theology is not merely a work of the intellect but also a gift of mystical wisdom granted by God to those blessed with **purity of heart**. In one of his famous hymns of divine love, he meditates on the **Blessed Trinity** in the context of celestial light:

> For the Three are one light, unique, not separable,
> but united in Three Persons without confusion.
> God is indeed completely indivisible by nature
> and by his essence is truly beyond every essence.
> He is not divided in power nor in form,
> nor in glory, nor in aspect,
> for he is contemplated completely as a simple light.

T

Tauler, John

(c. 1300-1361) Born in Strasbourg and also buried there, Tauler entered the Dominican Order in 1315, received an excellent education, and spent his entire life in towns and villages along the Rhine. He lived during a time of great turmoil in the Church and in the Empire. The pope was in exile in Avignon, famine and plague ravished the Continent, and new lay movements like the Beguines, the Brethren of the Free Spirit, and the Friends of God were on the rise.

Tauler favored the mystical life as taught by **Meister Eckhart** with its stress on the indwelling Trinity and imageless contemplation, but he also preached about the beauty of the active life with **devotion** to Christ's poverty as an antidote to vanity and worldliness. To Eckhart's teaching on the interior life, Tauler brought a balanced appreciation of prayer in practice, of the right blend of activity and abandonment, revealing the affective and practical side of mystical theology. In this way he avoided the excesses of **quietism**. He never doubted the importance of **asceticism** as the virtuous foundation of **mysticism** and the need to practice the **charity** that flows from **contemplation**.

For this reason Tauler, who underwent an interior **conversion** in his middle years, felt at home with a Flemish contemporary of his, **Blessed John Ruysbroeck,** whom he met in the Netherlands. He also had an influence on mystics of later ages, notably **Saint John of the Cross** and **Saint Teresa of Avila**. More than eighty of his transcribed sermons are considered to be authentically his. By avoiding rhetorical effect and intellectual subtlety, he was able to make his points in a down-to-earth way that explains why his sermons have survived the test of time.

Tauler preached, for example, on the five wounds of Christ as enabling believers to escape from the five prisons of: inordinate love for creatures, self-love, overattachment to reason, dependence on religious feelings and visionary experiences, and self-will. He held that before ascending to God one must descend in **humility** to the foot of the cross, imitating Christ's self-emptying, **detachment**, and abandonment to the will of the Father.

The mystery of the **Blessed Trinity** with its superabundant unity drew forth some of Tauler's most profound reflections. Its "imageless Image," he says, dwells in the inmost ground of the soul. Here we find by grace what

God possesses by nature. That is why over a lifetime of fidelity to God's Word, we should "allow the Holy Trinity to be born in the center of [our] soul, not by the use of human reason, but in essence and in truth; not in words, but in reality."

Teresa Benedicta of the Cross, Saint

(1891-1942) Jewish by birth and Catholic by **faith**, Saint Teresa, also known as Edith Stein, was born in Breslau, Germany, on Yom Kippur, the Day of Atonement. She was a woman gifted with a philosophical mind and a writer's heart, becoming at the University of Freiburg an assistant to Professor Edmund Husserl, the founder of the phenomenological movement.

In 1922, when Edith was studying for her doctorate, she met a fellow Jew, Jesus Christ, and he changed her life forever. To her mother's great sadness, she decided to enter the Church. For the next ten years she continued to teach and write, achieving such a high degree of excellence that she was offered a professorship at the University of Muenster. The following year the Nazis came to power. Many of her scholarly endeavors had to be curtailed, but this no longer disturbed her because she had set her heart on entering the cloistered Carmelite convent in Cologne. The person who inspired her to do so was her namesake, **Saint Teresa of Avila**. It was reading the *Book of Her Life* that led Edith to become a Catholic.

When Edith entered the convent, it seemed to her family that she was betraying them and her people in their hour of greatest need. But Edith recognized that to be a Carmelite was not to escape from life but to offer one's life to God, as the Lamb did, to bring spiritual comfort and **hope** to his people. For her the mystery of the cross was the one guarantee that the suffering of this life, no matter how horrific, can be united with the suffering of the Crucified Christ.

Edith knew that nothing could protect her from the Nazi's hatred of the Jews, certainly not a convent grille. She tells us in her journals and letters that she prayed that God would accept her life and her death in expiation for people's disbelief, for the salvation of Germany, and for world peace. A mere eight years after her profession in 1935 her life would achieve its goal of self-surrender and the cross.

When the Gestapo started persecuting religious orders in Cologne, Edith transferred to the Carmel in Echt, Holland. It was to no avail. In retaliation for a letter read by the Dutch bishops protesting the deportation of

Dutch Jews, the Nazis rounded up Catholics of Jewish origin and sent them to concentration camps in July 1942. Edith and Rosa Stein were among them. Her words to her sister were, "Come, Rosa, let us go for our people." The death of this prophetic witness to the sacredness of life occurred in Auschwitz on August 9, 1942.

Saint Teresa Benedicta of the Cross was canonized on October 11, 1998. These are her immortal words of inspiration to all believers:

> Whatever did not fit in with my plan did lie within the plan of God. I have an ever deeper and firmer belief that nothing is merely an accident when seen in the light of God, that my whole life down to the smallest details has been marked out for me in the plan of Divine Providence and has a completely coherent meaning in God's all-seeing eyes. And so I am beginning to rejoice in the light of glory wherein this meaning will be unveiled to me.

Teresa of Avila, Saint

(1515-82) In her early teens Teresa lost her mother and fell under the spell of a frivolous cousin who cultivated, instead of the **devotion** to which she aspired, vain and worldly ways that would haunt the future saint for years to come. Though attending a convent school directed by Augustinian nuns helped to reawaken her religious fervor, including the question of a vocation, she put off her decision. The time did come when, against her father's wishes, she entered the Monastery of the Incarnation in her hometown of Avila.

By 1537 she had professed her vows, but without the joy she expected to feel. Instead she became severely ill. The faith healer to whom she was sent nearly killed her. She fell into a deathlike coma and was almost buried alive! Paralysis overtook her. Though she returned to the convent, it was not to the business of the day but to the infirmary.

In 1542, as she tells us in the *Book of Her Life*, Saint Joseph cured her and she was able to walk again, but over the next twelve years, much to her shame, she resumed her old ways and became, in accordance with the customs of her convent, a "parlor favorite," caught in particular friendships and conversations more worldly than godly. All that was soon to change. Already, reading the *Confessions* of **Saint Augustine** had left her dissolved in tears, but during Lent of 1554, while meditating before a statue depicting Jesus' scourging at the pillar, she received the grace of radical **conversion**. Two years later, her spiritual betrothal to Christ took place followed by other mystical events, including that of the wound of love that made God the great passion of her life. Some of her friends and confessors concurred that she might be the victim of demonic delusion, but Teresa knew this was not so. In 1560 she began to compose her autobiography and to open herself without hesitation to God's leading. As she writes, "I understood that if the Lord didn't show me, I was able to learn little from books, because there was nothing I understood until his Majesty gave me understanding through experience..."

With a daring that would have been impossible without divine intervention, she chose to return to the original rule of Mount Carmel and to live the life of a reformed or Discalced ("without shoes") cloistered Carmelite in the utter **poverty** of the Convent of Saint Joseph in Avila. (See **Carmelite Spirituality**.) Several daughters followed their "Mother," and the instructions she gave them can be found most notably in her book *The Way of Perfection.*

Starting in 1567, she was authorized to found other monasteries, which meant that at her age she had to travel the rough roads of Spain, negotiate with landholders for property, raise considerable funds, and overcome incredible opposition and misunderstanding. Teresa's courage and cheerful heart prevailed over all obstacles, and new convents arose, including one at Medina del Campo, where she met at last the friar who would understand her call and her spiritual life and who would join her in the reform, **Saint John of the Cross**.

From 1574 to 1576, she established new convents in Segovia, Beas, and Seville, escaped denunciation by the Inquisition, and coped with many persecutions directed at her order. These events strained her already fragile health and caused her much anxiety. And yet at the epicenter of the controversy, in 1579, she wrote her greatest book, *The Interior Castle.*

Her strength waned severely in 1580, when her warrior heart began to fail. She received the last sacraments on October 3, and the next evening she met "his Majesty," Christ Jesus, whom she so loved and adored. Teresa was canonized in 1622. On September 27, 1970, Pope Paul VI proclaimed her a Doctor of the Church, the first woman to be so honored.

Thérèse of Lisieux, Saint

(1873-97) The youngest child of Louis and Zélie Martin, Marie-Françoise Thérèse moved from Alençon, France, her birthplace, to Lisieux in 1877, after the death of her mother. Her older sister, Pauline, became Marie-Françoise, Thérèse's second mother. The family settled themselves at Les Buissonnets in comfortable surroundings that contrasted with the inner turmoil this young woman was to experience for the next eight years.

Thérèse describes the winter of 1883 as a time of great trial. Pauline had already entered the Carmel at Lisieux. Thérèse began to experience continual headaches and insomnia. She got so sick that she went into convulsions, accompanied by nervous trembling, hallucinations, and comas. Then suddenly on May 13, the Feast of Pentecost, while she was praying before a statue of Our Lady of Victory, she said that the smile of the **Blessed Virgin Mary** cured her.

Spiritual trials followed these physical ones, though Thérèse was deeply consoled when she received her First Communion in May of 1884, followed in June by the sacrament of **Confirmation**. A year later Thérèse experienced liberation from the scruples that had plagued her for so long. Then on December 25, 1886, following Midnight Mass, she received the grace of her complete **conversion**. **Charity** entered her soul and she ceased thinking of herself. She saw as her mission the care of others. Shortly thereafter, as she prayed before a picture of the Crucified Christ, she experienced a burning thirst for souls and the need to pour out upon them his redeeming blood.

At the age of fifteen Thérèse received special permission to enter Carmel after the bold request she made to this effect of Pope Leo XIII. Her first "convert" was the prisoner Henri Pranzini, a convicted murderer, who embraced the cross prior to his execution. This event seemed to confirm what Thérèse would spend the rest of her life perfecting—an apostolic **mysticism** that she later named her little way of **spiritual childhood**. The name she chose to symbolize her new identity in Carmel beautifully expresses the **charism** of her life: Thérèse of the Child Jesus and the Holy Face.

Though she had only nine more years to live before tuberculosis would claim her, Thérèse taught all her sisters, including Céline (who was also in Carmel), the novices under her charge, and later the tens of thousands of people who embraced her as their strongest advocate in heaven how to live a life of joyful **abandonment to Divine Providence**, how to turn even the smallest daily event into an occasion of grace, and how to change the darkest trial of suffering into a time of intense mystical transformation.

A prolific letter writer and an exquisite poet, Thérèse agreed, under **obedience** to her superiors, to write her autobiography, never knowing that it would become one of the most inspiring and best loved books of all ages with its classic Christian doctrine of the little way. In it she vowed to spend her heaven as she had spent her time on earth: rescuing souls for Jesus.

Though Thérèse never left the enclosure, she became the patroness of the missions of the whole world. She who saw herself as a grain of sand in the immensity of the ocean was, in the words of Pope Pius X, "the greatest saint of modern times." On World Mission Sunday, October 19, 1998, Pope John Paul II named Thérèse a Doctor of the Church. She is only the third woman, after **Saint Teresa of Avila** and **Saint Catherine of Siena,** to be accorded this singular honor.

Thomas à Kempis

(1379-1471) Thomas was a major figure in a grass-roots religious revival movement in the Netherlands known as ***Devotio Moderna*** that flourished on the continent in the fourteenth century. One of its founders was Gerard Groote (1340-84), whose influence can be felt in the life and works of Thomas. Thomas entered a monastic community (Mount Saint Agnes in Holland) seeped in the teaching of the modern devotion. After his ordination to the priesthood in 1413, he became subprior of the monastery and later novice master.

Though in à Kempis' time theological speculation and intellectual argumentation occupied the minds of many clerics and academics, the common folk hungered for a return to moral and spiritual values, to the practice of genuine piety, to less stress on abstract information about the **faith** and more on lived formation in the faith. The Brethren of the Common Life, an association founded by Groote, answered their needs. Their **charism** was Christocentric, awe-filled yet in touch with everyday life; their spirit was more affective than speculative, fostering a love for virtue rooted in a wise blend of **solitude** and service.

Widely accepted as the author of *The Imitation of Christ*, it was Thomas who brought this **devotion** to the universal attention of the Church. In fact, this classic has been dubbed, after the Bible, the most read text in Christendom. Its perennial popularity is due in great measure to its lucid presentation of a trustworthy pattern of discipleship. Its chapters counsel seekers who want to follow the royal road of the cross to take Christ at his word.

This way of discipleship, treated specifically in Book One, begins with growth in self-knowledge through **humility,** combined with a progressive **detachment** from mere worldly values. Book Two focuses on how to find the kingdom of God within our own hearts and how to exercise **charity**. A dialogue between the soul and Jesus, its Beloved, offers much inner **consolation** in Book Three. Finally, Book Four focuses on the Blessed Sacrament and the reverence with which the **Eucharist** should be received since it places us in the presence of the living God and calls to mind his sacrifice of love for us.

Throughout the *Imitation*, Thomas derides what he calls "loveless scholarship," learning that only puffs a person up with his or her own importance but does not feed the interior life or assist in service to one's neighbor. He says, "Search for truth in holy writings, not eloquence." He teaches that all holy writings should be read in the same spirit with which they were written and that we should allow the love of pure truth to attract us. It profits us more to pay attention to what is said than to whether it is said in a lofty manner. À Kempis reminds us many times over that "people pass away, but the truth of the Lord endures forever."

Thomas Aquinas, Saint

(1225-74) An outstanding philosopher and theologian, the man who would eventually be named "Angelic Doctor of the Church" became not a Benedictine monk, as his Southern Italian parents expected, but a member of the Dominican Order of Preachers. His teacher, Saint Albert the Great (c. 1200-1280), saw that his brilliant student was not only a genius but also a lover of truth. Nothing satisfied him but the pursuit of intellectual excellence. For Thomas Aquinas, that meant setting his heart and mind wholly on God.

Though Thomas was by nature taciturn, some classmates in Cologne even dubbed him a "dumb ox." But in due time his "summa" of the **faith** would be known throughout the Christian world and would become required reading in Catholic seminary education. Thomas studied and began writing at the University of Paris, where he had attained his doctorate. Almost from the start, his new critical methods of theological disputation, combined with an appeal to orthodoxy, drew fire. He began to write his masterpiece, *Summa Theologica*, in 1266; it would become the most comprehensive exposition of the Catholic faith ever composed. He wrote it as a series of interlocking questions so as to demonstrate in a systematic and logical fashion the link between reason and revelation.

The entire Christian world owes a debt of gratitude to Aquinas for bringing our faith tradition into dialogue with the pre-Christian worldviews of Plato and Aristotle that were permeating Western thought. Thomas already believed that **contemplation** was a question of the ascent of the mind to God, aided by such basic ways of human thought as metaphysical speculation. The intellect at its highest level could only be enlightened by divine revelation and the inspiration of the Holy Spirit. The goal of all thought is to know God, be it only through a glass darkly (1 Corinthians 13:12), so as to serve him and others with a love that mirrors the self-emptying of Christ.

This desire may explain why suddenly, in 1273, Thomas ceased writing the *Summa*. He was graced with a religious experience so overwhelming, so intense and real, that it caused him to threaten to destroy his own life's labor. He said that compared to what he had seen, his *Summa* was only "so much straw." Thomas died when he was forty-nine, confessing that the **peace** he felt was the surest sign that after all his intellectual struggles on earth he would meet the price of his redemption in heaven. A few days prior to his death, he said, "I have taught and written in the faith of Jesus Christ and of the holy Roman Church, to whose judgment I offer and submit everything."

Trinity Whom I Adore

O my God, Trinity whom I adore, help me forget myself entirely so to establish myself in you, unmovable and peaceful as if my soul were already in eternity. May nothing be able to trouble my peace or make me leave you, O my unchanging God, but may each minute bring me more deeply into your mystery! Grant my soul peace. Make it your heaven, your beloved dwelling and the place of your rest. May I never abandon you there, but may I be there, whole and entire, completely vigilant in my faith, entirely adoring, and wholly given over to your creative action.

–*Saint Elizabeth of the Trinity*

Unceasing Prayer

To pray unceasingly is to live in **worship**, adoration, and awe. It is not merely a question of saying prayers, but of oneself becoming a living prayer. To pray unceasingly is not an experience reserved for a holy elite, but a way to physical, functional, and spiritual wholeness.

Saint Bernard of Clairvaux compares such prayer to a reservoir of divine energy continually being refilled inside of us, enabling us to share its power with others in the world. We meet God in a sunrise, a smiling face, an inspiring text. We detect in unexpected quarters, like a hospital bed, his providential care. We realize that the dross of human fallibility covers the gold of human dignity. We sense God's presence in an aging parent, a sick child, a crippled beggar—in all who are suffering, vulnerable, imperfect. When viewed from this perspective, the world becomes not a place where people fight for survival but a house of prayer. What is around and within us, the most ordinary appearances, become openings to God.

To pray without ceasing (1 Thessalonians 5:17) does not mean mumbling prayers from dawn to dusk. It means converting our very thought process into a prayer process or a continual conversation with God. A contemporary spiritual writer, **Henri J.M. Nouwen**, says that "prayer can eventually become unceasing ... when all our thoughts—beautiful and ugly, high and low, prideful and shameful, sorrowful and joyful—can be thought in the presence of God." In this way, Nouwen adds, "we move from a self-centered monologue to a God-centered dialogue."

Union in Love

Just as disobedience leads to breaking the commandments and to separation from him who gave them, so obedience leads to keeping the commandments and to union with him who gave them. Thus he who through obedience has kept the commandments has achieved righteousness and, moreover, he has not cut himself off from union in love with him who gave them; and the opposite is equally true.

–Saint Maximus the Confessor

Unitive Way (Union)
If the **purgative way** is a gift of grace given to us by God to disclose the **poverty** of our existence, and the **illuminative way** prepares us for still greater **detachment** from all that separates us from God, then the way of transforming union or unifying transformation draws us to the heart of the Triune God, who alone can satisfy our spiritual hunger.

While in the earlier stages of the spiritual life touches of union were brief but intense, at this more advanced stage they are enduring and life transforming. A person so graced may be aware of the divine indwelling of the **Blessed Trinity** in one's soul. Stirrings of profound tenderness might be accompanied by the courage to perform in Christ's name deeds requiring heroic virtue.

In *The Spiritual Canticle*, **Saint John of the Cross** explains that in the unitive way, love flows between God and the soul in a manner that produces, in his words, "abundant mystical understanding." As one moves from knowing about God to actually knowing and loving him, one comes to understand through faith what cannot be grasped through human faculties. Union with God cannot be attained by desire, imagination, intellect, or any other sense—not by anything known by means of human ingenuity or experience.

The way of union is truly the "way of unknowing" or the *via negativa*. All that we can feel and taste of God in this life is infinitely distant from him. We must pass beyond everything comprehensible to the incomprehensible. As a consequence, souls at this stage of the spiritual journey move from self-emptying to transformation in Christ, from **contemplation** to **charity**, from **solitude** to solidarity.

This phase of deepening—as distinct from the beginner's path of spiritual courtship and the proficient's of spiritual betrothal—is likened to spiritual marriage, which is the highest aspiration of souls seeking the endpoint of the way of perfection. As the darkness of unknowing overtakes the intellect of the lover, **faith** in the Beloved carries the bride-soul into the currents of mystical knowledge God wants to impart to her. As a result, her will is inflamed with affective longing and enkindled with renewed fervor. The will becomes, to use Saint John's metaphor, like a living flame of love, afire with transcendent knowledge.

Van Kaam, Adrian

(1920-) This modern-day spiritual master, research professor, and author was born in the Netherlands on April 19, 1920. In his teaching and writing, and by virtue of his personal witness, van Kaam engages his students and others in both ecumenical and interfaith dialogue.

In the last year of World War II, during the infamous Dutch Hunger winter of deprivation and deportation, van Kaam, then a theology student, helped Jews and Christians to hide in the Hague, his city of birth, and in Nieuwkoop, a village in the countryside where he published an underground journal. The young theology student brought **spiritual direction** and **consolation** to these hungry souls as they provided him with an unforgettable experiential basis for his research in the science, art, and discipline of formative spirituality.

Some years after the war and following his ordination to the priesthood, van Kaam was appointed professor of philosophy at his seminary. At the same time, he accepted an invitation to teach in local mills and factories in a nationwide program devoted to the social and spiritual formation of young laborers. This unique program was initiated during the war by the Belgian school supervisor Ms. Maria Schouwenaars; she and van Kaam worked together to implement a way of integrating faith and life in the light of his formation theology.

Shortly after completing his research and teaching assignments in the Netherlands, van Kaam was invited to join the psychology faculty of Duquesne University, in Pittsburgh, in 1954. There he was asked to develop a new type of program he named "psychology as a human science." At the same time, he was able to continue his research and writing in the field of formation.

In 1963, van Kaam founded the Institute of Man (later renamed the Institute of Formative Spirituality) at Duquesne University, where he launched the master's and doctoral programs in this field. He taught in the Institute as a research professor until the mid 1990s. By this time more than nine hundred students from around the world had been trained in formative spirituality at the Institute.

Van Kaam continues to be actively involved in the research, archival, publication, consultation, and formation work of the Epiphany Association as it ministers to the laity, clergy, and religious of many different faith groupings. Along with the service he offers to many under the auspices of the Association, van Kaam lectures in the United States and throughout the world. He also conducts seminars, conferences, and outreach programs sponsored by the Epiphany Academy of Formative Spirituality.

In addition to his eight-volume masterwork on formation science, anthropology, and theology, van Kaam is the author and coauthor with Susan Muto of many other books. He is also a prolific poet whose life work may be summarized in these few lines:

> May I sing to people
> About the mystery they deeply are,
> About the Spirit in their plodding lives.
> Already the fields are white
> Ready for the harvest.
> But few are the laborers
> To gather your chosen ones
> In the granary of the Spirit,
> To separate the golden grain
> Of their graced destiny
> From the straw of attachment.
>
> Lord, send me out into the fields
> And when I have done all I could
> Remind me kindly that I was only
> A useless servant.

Vianney, Saint John

(1786-1859) Commonly known as the Curé of Ars, Vianney was born in Lyons, France, shortly before the French Revolution. He was never much of a student, but because of his good will the Church decided to ordain him in 1815. He was missioned a few years later to a rather nondescript village to serve as the parish priest of Ars-en-Dombes. The people there were singularly uninterested in God or religion, but this did not deter their pastor. They were the blessed recipients of his **devotion** to prayer, his fasting, and his trust in God's **mercy**.

Legend has it that a pilgrim who visited Ars said to the Curé, "I have done so many bad things that God could not forgive me."

The saint replied forcefully, "To speak in this manner is blasphemy. It puts a road block before God's mercy and there are none. His mercy is infinite!"

The results of Saint John's ministry exceeded everyone's expectations. He became so renowned as a confessor and a preacher that from 1830 to 1845, hundreds of visitors and pilgrims came to Ars every day. People knew their pastor was a saint before he died. In **humility** John gave the credit for his ministry to Jesus, the Good Shepherd, upon whose mercy he relied in life as in death.

Vincent de Paul, Saint

(1580-1660) Vincent was born in France, the son of a peasant family. At first Vincent followed his own ambitions more than divine aspirations. Wanting to move up in the world, he pursued a university education and a call to the priesthood; he was ordained at the early age of nineteen.

While working in the household of the queen as a chaplain, he came under the influence of one of the masters of the **French School of Spirituality**, Pierre (later Cardinal) de Bérulle, and soon became a changed man. Vincent would find his fame not in courtly contacts but in care for the poor. He who had once refused to see his own father because of the man's tattered garb soon organized groups to provide the destitute with food and clothing.

In 1625 Vincent established a new congregation in the Church, the Vincentians, men of God under religious orders, who were devoted to advancing the formation of parish priests and to working in rural areas where good confessors were badly needed. So inspiring was Monsieur Vincent, as he was called, that wealth poured in to support his projects. People of means loved him as much as the poor.

Before long his influence had spread from France to the entire continent of Europe. He organized a variety of charitable services, to which he attracted the help of a widow who became Saint Louise de Marillac, with whom he founded the Daughters of Charity. Their network of service to the poor, notably through the establishment of hospitals, orphanages, and shelters for the physically and mentally infirm and for the homeless, would eventually span the world.

At the time of his death, Monsieur Vincent's congregation numbered five hundred priests. He had instructed them, as well as the sisters, to think of the poor as their masters. They themselves had to be effective servants, showing their love in concrete deeds, not romantic ideals. In one of his conferences to the Daughters we read: "May this spirit then always be apparent, when you go out and return; let the spirit of **charity**, **humility** and great simplicity be ever visible and never make use of artifice or cunning. If you live in this spirit, my dear Sisters, ah! how happy the Institute of Charity will be, how you will honor it, how it will be multiplied!"

Saint Vincent's legacy as the patron of charitable societies lives on in a special way in the Vincent de Paul Society, founded in 1833 by Frederic Ozanam, and in the services offered in parishes everywhere by the Ladies of Charity.

Vocal Prayer

The *Catechism* defines prayer that takes flesh, prayer put into words spoken aloud or verbalized internally, as vocal [2700]. This type of prayer is an essential part of Christian living. It can be either rote or spontaneous. Jesus used both forms. He instructed his disciples to pray the **Lord's Prayer,** and he blessed those who listened to his Sermon on the Mount. He prayed with words from the Old Testament, and he sought new expressions of praise. He rejoiced in the goodness of life, and he turned to his Father in heaven during his agony in the garden, beseeching him, if it were his will, to let this cup pass. Now his prayer, "Thy will be done," has become ours every time we recite the Our Father.

Vocal prayer allows us to embody our longing for God as when the psalmist prays, "Hearken to my words, O LORD, /attend to my sighing. /Heed my call for help, /my king and my God!" (Psalm 5:2-3). It involves our senses as when **Saint Francis of Assisi** prayed his Canticle to the Sun. It gives us an occasion to translate what we are feeling—joy and sorrow, elation and depletion, thanksgiving and lamentation—externally, without embarrassment, fully confident that prayers welling up from the heart are heard by God.

As the *Catechism* says, "We must pray with our whole being to give all power possible to our supplication" [2702]. Vocal prayer respects the fact that we are spirit-in-the-flesh. Hands and face, lips and arms, eyes and ears are bodily expressions of interior prayer. We read in the Book of Exodus about the battle between Israel and Amalek: "As long as Moses kept his hands raised up, Israel had the better of the fight, but when he let his hands rest, Amalek had the better of the fight" (Exodus 17:11). So tired did Moses' arms become that Aaron and Hur had to support them, but his prayers were answered and Joshua slew the enemy.

Prayer of this sort is powerful and passionate. It gives God the perfect worship he deserves in spirit and in truth. Vocal prayer is as effective prayed alone as it is in groups. It is not meant to take the place of interior or **contemplative prayer** but to create a trust and familiarity between us and God. The matter of vocal prayer is our daily life itself, its common experiences and ecclesial celebrations, especially the Holy Mass where we vocalize our prayers in the assembly of the faithful. A beautiful shared prayer is, "Lord, I am not worthy to receive you, but only say the word and I shall be healed."

Vocation to Love

Considering the mystical body of the Church, I had not recognized myself in any of the members described by St. Paul, or rather I desired to see myself in them *all.* Charity gave me the key to my *vocation.* I understood that if the Church had a body composed of different members, the most necessary and most noble of all cannot be lacking to it, and so I understood that the Church *had a Heart and that this Heart was BURNING WITH LOVE. I understood it was Love alone* that made the Church's members act, that if *Love* ever became extinct, apostles would not preach the Gospel and martyrs would not shed their blood. I understood that LOVE COMPRISED ALL VOCATIONS, THAT LOVE WAS EVERYTHING, THAT IT EMBRACED ALL TIMES AND PLACES ... IN A WORD, THAT IT WAS ETERNAL!

Then, in the excess of my delirious joy, I cried out: O Jesus, my Love ... my *vocation*, at last I have found it ... MY VOCATION IS LOVE!

–Saint Thérèse of Lisieux

Will of God

To submit our own wills, freely and out of love, to the will of God is an act not even God can compel. This submission unites us as nothing else can to God's eternal plan and purpose for our life. The divine will is in complete harmony with God's holiness, righteousness, goodness, and truth. Jesus himself said, "Whoever does the will of God is my brother and sister and mother" (Mark 3:35).

To follow the will of God is less a matter of "willpower" and more a way of life—a loving orientation of our whole being to what "is good and pleasing and perfect" (Romans 12:2). For the apostle Paul, to seek and find, to acknowledge and obey, the Father's will is to rise from the slavery of sin to the freedom of the children of God. For what else does the Father will but our holiness? What else does he wish than that we refrain from immorality (cf. 1 Thessalonians 4:3)?

The ultimate outcome of living in **obedience** to God's will is a loving and grateful heart. Paul says, "In all circumstances give thanks, for this is the will of God for you in Christ Jesus" (1 Thessalonians 5:18). He also writes in his Letter to the Ephesians that "[God] has made known to us the mystery of his will in accord with his favor that he set forth in him as a plan for the fullness of times, to sum up all things in Christ, in heaven and on earth" (Ephesians 1:9-10).

As we submit each facet of our lives to the will of God, we receive abundant graces in return. Our love-will enables us not only to act in Jesus' name but to endure the cross as he did, confident that we shall rise with him even as we die for him. For Jesus, doing the will of the Father was his food and his drink. He teaches us in the **Lord's Prayer** to say in all places and under all circumstances, "Not my will but yours be done" (Luke 22:42).

William of Saint Thierry

(1085-1148) A man of noble parentage, William was born in Liege, France, but left there to study at Rheims. Thanks to his education and social standing, he could have pursued a worldly career, but he chose instead to enter the nearby Benedictine monastery of Saint Thierry around 1121. An admirer of **Saint Gregory of Nyssa** and the Greek Fathers in the East, as well as of **Saint Augustine of**

Hippo in the West, William was able to synthesize the best of both worlds in his theological works on the knowledge and love of God. He served as the abbot of his monastery for about fourteen years, providing exemplary discipline and spiritual leadership.

During this time there developed between him and **Saint Bernard of Clairvaux** a close and lasting friendship, which was influential in William's decision to become a monk of the Order of Cistercians of the Strict Observance. In 1135, he resigned his abbatial office and withdrew to the meditative life of the **Cistercian** monastery of Signy. There he devoted most of his time to writing due to an illness that left him unable to perform manual labor.

It was at Signy that William composed his masterworks on the integration of belief and loving surrender to God: *The Enigma of Faith* and *The Mirror of Faith*. But writing had always been an important part of William's life. Prior to this prolific period, he had written while in office his books *The Nature and Dignity of Love* and *On Contemplating God*; numerous treatises on the writings of the Fathers and Doctors of the Church; and, in addition to his *Prayers* and *Meditations*, a commentary on the Song of Songs.

In 1144, after visiting the **Carthusian** monks of Mont-Dieu near Rheims, he composed *The Golden Epistle*, one of the most significant medieval works on the value of the contemplative life. With its insights into *lectio divina*, the formative reading of Holy Scripture, and **spiritual direction**, this letter contains a wealth of ascetic and mystical wisdom. However, William's main interest was living the **faith**, not theological debate. He proposed that the soul, although estranged from God due to original sin, is also empowered by grace to experience a mystical return to its divine origin during its earthly existence.

According to William, as humans are progressively liberated from material and temporal impediments to union, eventually we may undergo, as God's gift, an experiential knowledge of him by a process of (1) *reminiscence* (the ascetic stage, relative to the Father); (2) *understanding* (the intellectual stage, relative to the Son); and (3) *love* (the unitive stage, relative to the Holy Spirit). William viewed our participation in the life of the **Blessed Trinity** as an anticipation of our eternal existence in the life to come. He died at Signy in 1148, convinced that once our will inclines to God in love, clings to him in union, and enjoys him in **charity**, we shall have found our way to heaven, in part at least already on this earth.

Work for Your Glory

O My God! Most Blessed Trinity, I desire to *Love* you and make you *loved*, to work for the glory of the Holy Church by saving souls on earth and liberating those suffering in purgatory. I desire to accomplish your will perfectly and to reach the degree of glory you have prepared for me in your kingdom. I desire, in a word, to be a saint, but I feel my helplessness and I beg you, O my God! to be yourself my *Sanctity*!

Since you loved me so much as to give me your only Son as my Savior and my Spouse, the infinite treasures of his merits are mine. I offer them to you with gladness, begging you to look upon me only in the Face of Jesus and in his heart burning with *Love*.

–*Saint Thérèse of Lisieux*

Worship

In the deepest sense, worship is a constellation of dispositions in which we recognize the infinite perfection of God, and offer to him alone our veneration, reverence, awe, and wonder. To worship anyone or anything other than God is to risk turning in on ourselves or remaining slaves to sin. That is why we are forbidden by the First Commandment to worship false gods or to pay homage to idols (cf. Deuteronomy 6:13).

According to the *Catechism*, "Adoration is the first act of the virtue of religion" [2096]. It is the humble acknowledgment on our part that God is our Lord and Savior. He is the Master; we, the disciples. He is the Creator; we, the creatures.

When we lead lives of worship, we can expect to become God-guided rather than self-centered people. The more we cultivate adoration as a lasting disposition of the heart, the more likely we are to stay focused on the Adored. By the same token, to worship or adore anyone or anything more than God is to shun the invitation to divine intimacy.

To worship God is to thank him for his mercy and love, to accept with submission our duty to obey his law, and to delight in his presence all the days of our lives.

Xavier, Saint Francis

(1506-52) When **Saint Ignatius of Loyola** established the Society of Jesus, he did so with several companions, of whom Francis Xavier was one. Francis was known for his wit and humor, his genius for learning, his good judgment, and his openness to new experiences—character traits that would suit him well in the years to come. First, however, he had to conquer the most dangerous enemy of all: his vainglory.

Performing Saint Ignatius' spiritual exercises had a powerful effect on the life of Francis Xavier. He found himself drawn day and night to the **contemplation** of heavenly things, complemented by profound sentiments of **compunction**. From these meditations he emerged a changed man, ready to be used by God for a special purpose.

After rigorous training and service to the poor, it was Francis' mission to launch the Jesuits' effort to go and preach to all nations. Far from his native land of Spain and his student days with Ignatius at the University of Paris, Francis spread the Word of God in Africa and Asia, most notably in Japan. He preached the word with such powerful **zeal** that in the course of just ten years Francis established the Church and brought Jesus Christ to a whole new world where multitudes were baptized and miracles were performed. However, Francis' fondest dream—evangelizing the people of China—never came to pass. He died en route to what he believed to be the grand prize of his tireless missionary efforts. Along with **Saint Thérèse of Lisieux,** he has been designated the patron saint of foreign missions.

X-Ray of Perfection

The thief who received the kingdom of heaven, though not as the reward of virtue, is a true witness to the fact that salvation is ours through the grace and mercy of God. All of our holy fathers knew this and all with one accord teach that perfection in holiness can be achieved only through humility. Humility, in its turn, can be achieved only through faith, fear of God, gentleness and the shedding of all possessions. It is by means of these that we attain perfect love, through the grace and compassion of our Lord Jesus Christ, to whom be glory through all ages. Amen.

–John Cassian

Yahweh

The name of God revealed to Moses, "I Am He Who Is" (cf. Exodus 3:13-15), or YHWH, reminds us that God is mystery. All we know of him from the revelation is but a reminder of all that we do not know. Out of respect and reverence, the Jews do not even utter the sacred name aloud [209].

The dispositions evoked in us by the hiddenness of God are awe and adoration. Though God's name is ineffable, the *Catechism* reminds us that God in his faithfulness remains ever close to us, "from everlasting to everlasting" [207].

Understanding the divine name, in keeping with the Church's tradition, leads us to proclaim that "God is the fullness of Being and of every perfection, without origin and without end." It follows that "all creatures receive all that they are and have from him; but he alone *is* his very being, and he is of himself everything that he is" [213].

Yes, Father

Let nothing disturb you,
Nothing dismay you.
All things are passing,
God never changes.
Patient endurance
Attains all things,
God alone suffices.

–Saint Teresa of Avila

Zeal

This virtue signifies the love of God in action. This ardent intensity applies to acts of **mercy** as well as to just punishments, as when God himself zealously intervened on behalf of the people of Israel. When pagan nations set out to alienate them from the Covenant, he defended his Chosen with boundless zeal. Their enemies were no match for the Lord, who dealt with them with holy anger, wrath, and fury.

Just as God's zeal aided Israel in her plight, so did it turn against her when she dared to worship false gods (Deuteronomy 29:15-20). So powerful a disposition can this be that the Scriptures confirm that "zeal for your house will consume me" (Psalm 69:10; cf. John 2:17) as it did Moses and David, Paul and Stephen, and many others.

Zeal in the pursuit of a cause like serving God needs to be couched in prudence. As Paul warned the Romans (10:2), zeal for God must be tempered with discernment. Before his conversion, Saul persecuted the Christians as earnestly as he afterward defended the gospel. He was a zealot through and through, but he had to direct this fiery virtue to its proper end. As **Saint Symeon the New Theologian** says, "Press on with greater zeal and courage in the practice of virtues, and be not faithless toward the words and teachings of your fathers in God."

One of these fathers is **Saint Bernard of Clairvaux**, who tells us in Sermon 18 of his eighty-six sermons on the Song of Songs that zeal is an infused virtue that draws us first and foremost to prayer. It arouses us at the start of our journey to God and draws us toward its loyal and courageous end. As Saint Bernard says:

> See how precious the graces that must first be infused, so that when we venture to pour them out we may dispense them from a spirit that is filled rather than impoverished. We need first of all **compunction** of heart, then fervor of spirit; thirdly, the labor of penance; fourthly, works of **charity**; fifthly, zeal for prayer; sixthly, leisure for **contemplation**; seventhly, love in all its fullness. All these are the work of one and the same Spirit, accomplished by the process called infusion; and, insofar as it has taken place, those services called effusion can be truly and hence safely performed to the praise and glory of our Lord, Jesus Christ, who with the Father and the same

Holy Spirit lives and reigns, God,
for ever and ever. Amen.

Index of Contents

Abandonment to Divine Providence . . . 11
Acquisition of the Holy Spirit 11
Aelred of Rievaulx, Saint 12, 13
Ambrose, Saint 12
Angelic Orders 13
Angels 14
Anselm of Canterbury, Saint 14, 125
Antony of Egypt, Saint 15
Apparitions 16
Arianism 16
Aridity. 17
Ascetic Practices 18
Asceticism 18
Athanasius of Alexandria, Saint. 19
Augustine of Hippo, Saint 19
Augustinian Spirituality 21

Baptism. 23
Basil the Great, Saint 23
Be Filled With Faithfulness. 24
Beatitudes 24
Bede the Venerable, Saint 25
Benedict of Nursia, Saint 26
Benedictine Spirituality 27
Bernadette of Lourdes, Saint 28
Bernard of Clairvaux, Saint 28
Blessed Trinity. 29
Bonaventure, Saint 30, 145
Bosco, Saint John 30

Cabrini, Saint Frances Xavier 33, 101
Call to Holiness. 33
Capital Sins 34
Carmelite Spirituality 35
Carthusian Spirituality 35
Cassian, John 36, 181
Catherine of Genoa, Saint 37
Catherine of Siena, Saint 38
Celibacy 39
Centering Prayer 40
Charism 40
Charismatic Spirituality 41
Charity 42
Chastity. 42
Cistercian Spirituality. 43
Ciszek, Father Walter. 44, 88
Clare of Assisi, Saint 45
Classics of Christian Spirituality 46
Clement of Alexandria, Saint 47
Climacus, John 47
Cloud of Unknowing, The. 48
Come, Spirit of Love 49
Communion of Saints 50
Compassion 51
Compunction 51
Confirmation 52
Consolations 53
Contemplation 54
Contemplative Prayer 55
Conversion 55
Cyprian of Carthage, Saint. 56
Cyril of Jerusalem, Saint 57

Dark Night of the Soul 59
Day, Dorothy 60, 132
Day of Judgment 60
De Caussade, Jean-Pierre. 61, 138
De Foucauld, Charles 62
De Montfort, Saint
Louis-Marie Grignon 62
Desert Experience 63
Desert Fathers. 64
Desolations 65
Detachment 65
Devils 66
Devotio Moderna 67
Devotion. 68
Discernment of Spirits 68

Distractions in Prayer . . . 69
Dominic, Saint . . . 70

Eckhart, Meister . . . 73, 128
Elizabeth of the Trinity, Saint . . . 74, 168
Encompassed by God . . . 75
Eucharist . . . 75
Eudes, Saint John . . . 76
Evagrius Ponticus . . . 77
Examination of Conscience . . . 77

Faith . . . 79
For Our Sake . . . 79
Forgiveness . . . 79
Francis de Sales, Saint . . . 80
Francis of Assisi, Saint . . . 81
Franciscan Spirituality . . . 82
French School of Spirituality . . . 83
Fruits of the Holy Spirit . . . 84

Gerson, John . . . 87
Gertrude the Great, Saint . . . 87
Gifts of the Holy Spirit . . . 88
God's Will . . . 88
Gregory Nazianzus, Saint . . . 89
Gregory of Nyssa, Saint . . . 89
Gregory the Great, Saint . . . 90
Guardian Angels . . . 91
Guigo II . . . 92

Hadewijch . . . 95
Hildegard of Bingen, Saint . . . 95
Hilton, Walter . . . 96
Holy Spirit of God . . . 97
Hope . . . 97
Hopkins, Gerard Manley . . . 97
Humility . . . 98

Ignatian Spirituality . . . 99
Ignatius of Loyola, Saint . . . 99
Illuminative Way . . . 100
Inspirations . . . 101
Irenaeus of Lyons, Saint . . . 101

Jerome, Saint . . . 103
Jesus Prayer . . . 104
John Chrysostom, Saint . . . 104
John of the Cross, Saint . . . 105
Joy in God . . . 107
Julian of Norwich . . . 107
Justice . . . 108

Know the Creed . . . 109
Kolbe, Saint Maximilian . . . 109
Kowalska, Saint Maria Faustina . . . 110

Ladder of Charity . . . 113
Lawrence of the Resurrection, Brother . 113
Libermann, Venerable Francis . . . 114
Liguori, Saint Alphonsus . . . 115
Liturgy . . . 115
Liturgy of the Hours . . . 116
Lord's Prayer, The . . . 116

Marie of the Incarnation, Blessed . . . 119
Mary, Blessed Virgin . . . 119
Maximus the Confessor, Saint . . . 120, 169
Mechthild of Magdeburg . . . 121
Meditation . . . 122
Mercy . . . 122
Merici, Saint Angela . . . 123
Merton, Thomas . . . 123
Mighty and Merciful God . . . 125
More, Saint Thomas . . . 125
Mysticism . . . 125

Neri, Saint Philip . . . 127
Never Stop Praying . . . 128
Newman, John Henry Cardinal . . 109, 128
Nicholas of Cusa, Bishop . . . 129
Nouwen, Henri J. M. . . . 130

Obedience . . . 131
One Step at a Time . . . 131
Origen . . . 132

Padre Pio, Blessed . . . 133
Peace . . . 134
Poverty of Spirit . . . 135
Prayer of Intercession . . . 136

Prayer of Petition 137
Prayer of Presence 138
Prayer of the Heart 138
Prompted by Pure Love 138
Pseudo-Dionysius 14, 139
Purgative Way 140
Purity of Heart 141

Queen Humility 143
Quietism 143

Restoring Grace 145
Richard of Saint Victor 145
Rolle, Richard 107, 146
Ruysbroeck, Blessed John 24, 146

Seton, Saint Elizabeth Ann 149
Silence 150
Solitude 151
Spiritual Childhood 151
Spiritual Direction 152
Spiritual Formation 153
Spiritual Friendship 154
Spiritual Reading as Art 155
Spiritual Reading as Discipline 156
Stein, Edith (*see Teresa Benedicta of the Cross, St.*)
Surrender to God 157
Suso, Blessed Henry 158
Symeon the New Theologian 159

Tauler, John 79, 161
Teresa Benedicta of the Cross, Saint . . . 162
Teresa of Avila, Saint 143, 163, 183
Thérèse of Lisieux, Saint . . . 166, 175, 179
Thomas à Kempis 60
Thomas Aquinas, Saint 167
Trinity Whom I Adore 168

Unceasing Prayer 169
Union in Love 169
Unitive Way 170

Van Kaam, Adrian 171
Vianney, Saint John 172
Vincent de Paul, Saint 173
Vocal Prayer 174
Vocation to Love 175

Will of God 177
William of Saint Thierry 177
Work for Your Glory 179
Worship 179

Xavier, Saint Francis 75, 181
X-Ray of Perfection 181

Yahweh 183
Yes, Father 183

Zeal 185

Bibliography

Aelred of Rievaulx, St. *Spiritual Friendship* in *Cistercian Fathers Series*, Volume 5. Trans. Mary Eugenia Laker. Washington, D.C.: Cistercian Publications, 1974.

à Kempis, Thomas. *The Imitation of Christ: A Timeless Classic for Contemporary Readers*. Trans. William C. Creasy. Notre Dame, Ind.: Ave Maria Press, 1989.

Albert and Thomas: Selected Writings in *The Classics of Western Spirituality*. Trans. Simon Tugwell. New York: Paulist Press, 1998.

Ambrose, St. *Seven Exegetical Works* in *The Fathers of the Church*, Volume 65. Trans. Michael P. McHugh. Washington, D.C.: Catholic University of America Press, 1972.

An Aquinas Reader: Selections from the Writings of Thomas Aquinas. Ed. Mary Clark. Garden City, N.Y.: Image Books, 1972.

Anonymous. *The Cloud of Unknowing* and *The Book of Privy Counseling*. Ed. William Johnston. New York: Doubleday Image Books, 1973.

Aquinas, Thomas, St. *Treatise on Happiness*. Trans. John A. Oesterle. Notre Dame, Ind.: University of Notre Dame Press, 1983.

Athanasius of Alexandria, St. *The Life of Antony and the Letter to Marcellinus* in *The Classics of Western Spirituality*. Trans. Robert C. Gregg. New York: Paulist Press, 1980.

Augustine, St. *The Trinity* in *The Fathers of the Church*, Volume 45. Trans. Stephen McKenna. Washington, D.C.: Catholic University of America Press, 1963.

Basil, St. *Exegetic Homilies* in *The Fathers of the Church*, Volume 46. Trans. Agnes Clare Way. Washington, D.C.: Catholic University of America Press, 1963.

Bede the Venerable, St. *Cistercian Studies Series.* Trans. David Hurst. Kalamazoo, Mich.: Cistercian Publications, 1983.

Beevers, John. *Storm of Glory: The Story of St. Thérèse of Lisieux.* Garden City, N.Y.: Doubleday, Image Books, 1955.

Bernard of Clairvaux: A Lover Teaching the Way of Love. Ed. M. Basil Pennington. Hyde Park, N.Y.: New City Press, 1997.

Bernard of Clairvaux: Selected Works in *The Classics of Western Spirituality.* Trans. G. R. Evans. New York: Paulist Press, 1987.

Bernard of Clairvaux, St. *On the Song of Songs I* in *Cistercian Fathers Series,* Volume 4. Trans. Kilian Walsh. Spencer, Mass.: Cistercian Publications, 1971.

Bérulle and the French School: Selected Writings in *The Classics of Western Spirituality.* Trans. Lowell M. Glendon, S.S. New York: Paulist Press, 1989.

Beumer, Jurgen. *Henri Nouwen: A Restless Seeking for God.* New York: Crossroad, 1997.

Bonaventure, St. *The Soul's Journey into God* in *The Classics of Western Spirituality.* Trans. Ewert Cousins. New York: Paulist Press, 1978.

Borriello, Luigi. *Spiritual Doctrine of Blessed Elizabeth of the Trinity.* Staten Island, N.Y.: Alba House, 1986.

Carthusian Spirituality: The Writings of Hugh of Balma and Guigo de Pointe in *The Classics of Western Spirituality.* Trans. Dennis D. Martin. New York: Paulist Press, 1997.

Cassian, John. *Conferences* in *The Classics of Western Spirituality.* Trans. Colm Luibheid. New York: Paulist Press, 1985.

Catechism of the Catholic Church. English Translation. Washington D.C.: United States Catholic Conference, Inc. 1994.

Catechism of the Catholic Church: Modifications from the "Editio Typica". English translation. Washington, D.C.: United States Catholic Conference, Inc., 1997.

Catherine of Genoa, St. *Purgation and Purgatory, The Spiritual Dialogue* in *The Classics of Western Spirituality.* Trans. Serge Hughes. New York: Paulist Press, 1979.

Catherine of Siena, St. *The Dialogue* in *The Classics of Western Spirituality.* Trans. Suzanne Noffke. New York: Paulist Press, 1980.

Celeste, Marie. *The Intimate Friendships of Elizabeth Ann Bayley Seton: First Native-Born American Saint (1774-1821).* Staten Island, N.Y.: Alba House, 1989.

Chittister, Joan D. *The Rule of Benedict: Insight for the Ages.* New York: Crossroad, 1996.

Ciszek, Walter J. with Daniel Flaherty. *He Leadeth Me.* San Francisco, Calif.: Ignatius Press, 1995.

Christian Spirituality: The Essential Guide to the Most Influential Spiritual Writings of the Christian Tradition. Ed. Frank N. Magill and Ian P. McGreal. San Francisco: Harper & Row, 1988.

Chrysostom, John, St. *On the Incomprehensible Nature of God* in *The Fathers of the Church*, Volume 72. Trans. Paul W. Harkins. Washington, D.C.: The Catholic University of America Press, 1982.

Cistercians and Cluniacs: The Case for Citeaux—A *Dialogue Between Two Monks, An Argument on Four Questions* in *Cistercian Fathers Series*, Volume 33. Kalamazoo, Mich.: Cistercian Publications, 1977.

Clark, Keith. *An Experience of Celibacy: A Creative Reflection on Intimacy, Loneliness, Sexuality and Commitment.* Notre Dame, Ind.: Ave Maria Press, 1982.

Clement of Alexandria, St. *Christ the Educator* in *The Fathers of the Church Series*, Volume 23. Trans. Simon P. Wood. Washington, D.C.: Catholic University of America Press, 1953.

Climacus, John. *The Ladder of Divine Ascent* in *The Classics of Western Spirituality.* Trans. Colm Luibheid and Norman Russell. New York: Paulist Press, 1982.

Confessions of St. Augustine. Trans. John K. Ryan. New York: Doubleday, Image Books, 1960.

The Collected Works of St. John of the Cross. Trans. Kieran Kavanaugh and Otilio Rodriguez. Washington, D.C.: Institute of Carmelite Studies, 1991.

The Collected Works of St. Teresa of Avila, Volume 1. Trans Kieran Kavanaugh and Otilio Rodriguez. Washington, D.C.: Institute of Carmelite Studies, 1976, 1987.

The Collected Works of St. Teresa of Avila, Volume 2. Trans. Kieran Kavanaugh and Otilio Rodriguez. Washington, D.C.: Institute of Carmelite Studies, Publications, 1980.

The Collected Works of St. Teresa of Avila, Volume 3. Trans. Kieran Kavanaugh and Otilio Rodriquez. Washington, D.C.: Institute of Carmelite Studies, Publications, 1985.

Connor, Edward D. *The Pentecostal Movement in the Catholic Church.* Notre Dame, Ind.: Ave Maria Press, 1971.

Craine, Renate. *Hildegard: Prophet of the Cosmic Christ.* New York: Crossroad, 1997.

Crosby, Michael H. *Spirituality of the Beatitudes: Matthew's Challenge for First World Christians.* Maryknoll, N.Y.: Orbis Books, 1981.

Cyprian, St. *Letters in The Fathers of the Church,* Volume 51. Trans. Rose Bernard Donna. Washington, D.C.: The Catholic University of America Press, 1964.

Day, Dorothy. *Selected Writings.* Ed. Robert Ellsberg. Maryknoll, N.Y.: Orbis Books, 1983.

Divine Mercy in My Soul: The Diary of the Servant of God: Sister M. Faustina Kowalska. Stockbridge, Mass.: Marian Press, 1987.

De Caussade, Jean-Pierre. *Abandonment to Divine Providence.* Trans. John Beevers. Garden City, N.Y.: Image Books, 1975.

De Foucauld, Charles. *Hope in the Gospels.* Hyde Park, N.Y.: New City Press, 1990.

DeMaria, Mother Saverio. *Mother Frances Xavier Cabrini.* Trans. Rose Basile Green. Chicago: Missionary Sisters of the Sacred Heart of Jesus, 1984.

Dessain, C.S. *Newman's Spiritual Themes.* Dublin, Ireland: Veritas Publications, 1977.

Dorothy Day Book: A Selection from Her Writings and Readings. Ed. Margaret Quigley and Michael Garvey. Springfield, Ill.: Templegate Publishers, 1982.

Egan, Harvey. *An Anthology of Christian Mysticism.* Collegeville, Minn.: The Liturgical Press. 1991.

Elizabeth of the Trinity. The Complete Works. Volume I. Trans. Aletheia Kane. Washington, D.C.: Institute of Carmelite Studies, 1984.

__. *The Complete Works.* Volume II. Trans. Anne Englund Nash, Washington, D.C.: Institute of Carmelite Studies, 1995.

Elizabeth Seton: Selected Writings in *Sources of American Spirituality.* Ed. Ellin Kelly and Annabelle Melville. New York: Paulist Press, 1987.

Ellsberg, Robert. *All Saints: Daily Reflections on Saints, Prophets, and Witnesses for Our Time.* New York: Crossroad, 1997.

The Epistles of St. Clement of Rome and St. Ignatius of Antioch in *Ancient Christian Writers.* Trans. James A. Kleist. Westminster, Md.: The Newman Press, 1946.

Evagrius Ponticus, *The Praktikos: Chapters on Prayer* in *Cistercian Studies Series,* Number Four. Trans. John Eudes Bamberger. Spencer, Mass.: Cistercian Publications, 1970.

Fairlie, Henry. *The Seven Deadly Sins Today.* Washington, D.C.: New Republic Books, 1978.

Francis and Clare: The Complete Works in *The Classics of Western Spirituality.* Trans. Regis J. Armstrong and Ignatius C. Brady. New York: Paulist Press, 1982.

Francis de Sales, St. *Introduction to the Devout Life.* Trans. John K. Ryan. Garden City, N.Y.: Image Books, 1972.

___. *Treatise on the Love of* God, Volume I. Trans. John K. Ryan. Rockford, Ill.: Tan Books, 1974.

___. *Treatise on the Love of God*, Volume II. Trans. John K. Ryan, Rockford, Ill.: Tan Books, 1974.

Francis de Sales and Jane de Chantal: Letters of Spiritual Direction in *The Classics of Western Spirituality.* Trans. Péronne Marie Thibert. New York: Paulist Press, 1988.

Francis of Assisi, St. *Omnibus of Sources: Writings and Early Biographies.* Ed. Marion A. Habig. Chicago: Franciscan Herald Press, 1973.

From Glory to Glory: Texts from Gregory of Nyssa's Mystical Writings. Trans. by Herbert Musurillo Crestwood, New York: St. Vladimir's Seminary Press, 1979.

Gerson, Jean. *Early Works* in *The Classics of Western Spirituality.* Trans. Brian Patrick McGuire. New York: Paulist Press, 1998.

Gertrude of Helfta, St. *The Herald of Divine Love* in *The Classics of Western Spirituality.* Trans. Margaret Winkworth. New York: Paulist Press, 1993.

Gregory of Nazianzus, St. *Three Poems Concerning His Own Affairs, Concerning Himself and the Bishops, Concerning His Own Life* in *The Fathers of the Church,* Volume 75. Trans. Denis Molaise Meehan. Washington, D.C.: The Catholic University of America, 1986.

Gregory of Nyssa: The Life of Moses in *The Classics of Western Spirituality.* Trans. Abraham J. Malherbe and Everett Ferguson. New York: Paulist Press, 1978.

Gregory of Nyssa, St. *The Lord's Prayer, The Beatitudes* in *Ancient Christian Writers.* Trans., Hilda C. Graef. Westminster, Md.: Newman Press, 1954.

Gregory the Great, St. *Pastoral Care* in *Ancient Christian Writers.* Trans. Henry Davis. New York: Newman Press, 1950.

Gruen, Anselm. *Heaven Begins Within You: Wisdom from the Desert Fathers.* New York: Crossroad, 1994.

Guardini, Romano. *The Lord's Prayer.* Manchester, N.H.: Sophia Institute Press, 1996.

Guigo II. *The Ladder of Monks and Twelve Meditations.* Trans. Edmund Colledge. Kalamazoo, Mich.: Cistercian Publications, 1981.

Hadewijch. *The Complete Works* in *The Classics of Western Spirituality.* Trans. Mother Columba Hart. New York: Paulist Press, 1980.

Hausherr, Irénée. *Penthos: The Doctrine of Compunction in the Christian East.* Trans. Anselm Hufstader, Kalamazoo, Mich.: Cistercian Publications. 1982.

Hildegard of Bingen in *The Classics of Western Spirituality.* New York: Paulist Press, 1990.

Hillyer, Philip. *Charles de Foucauld: The Way of the Christian Mystics.* Collegeville, Minn.: Liturgical Press, 1990.

Hilton, Walter. *The Stairway of Perfection.* Trans. M.L. Del Mastro. Garden City, N.Y.: Image Books, 1979.

Hopkins, Gerard Manley. *Poems and Prose* in *Everyman's Library.* New York: Alfred A. Knopf, 1995.

Jesus Living in Mary: Handbook of the Spirituality of St. Louis Marie de Montfort. Eds. Patrick Gaffney and Richard Payne. Bay Shore, N.Y.: Montfort Publications, 1994.

John of Ruysbroeck. Trans. C.A. Wynschenk. Westminster, Md.: Christian Classics, 1974.

Julian of Norwich. *Showings* in *The Classics of Western Spirituality.* Trans. Edmund Colledge. New York: Paulist Press, 1978.

Kelly, J.N.D. *Golden Mouth: The Story of John Chrysostom—Ascetic, Preacher, Bishop.* Grand Rapids, Mich.: Baker Books, 1995.

Kluz, Ladislaus. *Kolbe and the Kommandant: Two Worlds in Collision.* Trans. M. Angela Santor. Stevensville, Mont.: DeSmet Foundation, 1983.

Lang, Judith. *The Angels of God: Understanding the Bible.* Hyde Park, N.Y.: New City Press, 1997.

Lappin, Peter. *Give Me Souls! Life of Don Bosco.* New Rochelle, N.Y.: Don Bosco Publications, 1977.

Lawrence of the Resurrection, Brother. *The Practice of the Presence of God.* Trans. Donald Attwater. Springfield, Ill.: Templegate, 1974.

The Letters of St. Jerome in *Ancient Christian Writers.* Trans. Charles Christopher Mierow. Westminster, Md.: The Newman Press, 1963.

Libermann, Francis. *Spiritual Letters to Clergy and Religious.* Three Volumes. Trans. Walter van de Putte. Pittsburgh, Pa.: Duquesne University, 1966.

___. *Spiritual Letters to People in the World.* Volume II. Trans. Walter van de Putte. Pittsurgh, Pa.: Duquesne University, 1963.

The Life of Mary as Seen by the Mystics. Compiled by Raphael Brown. Rockford, Ill.: Tan Books, 1951.

Light from Light: An Anthology of Christian Mysticism. Ed. Louis Depré and James A. Wiseman. New York: Paulist Press, 1988.

Lives of the Desert Fathers. Trans. Norman Russell. Kalamazoo, Mich.: Cistercian Publications, 1980.

Louf, André. *The Cistercian Way.* Trans. Nivard Kinsella. Kalamazoo, Mich.: Cistercian Publications, 1983.

Maryknoll Catholic Dictionary. Ed. Albert J. Nevins, M.M. Denville, N.J.: Dimension Books, 1964.

McGinn, Bernard. *The Doctors of the Church: Thirty-Three Men and Women Who Shaped Christianity.* New York: Crossroads, 1999.

McNeill, Donald P., Douglas A. Morrison, Henri J.M. Nouwen. *Compassion: A Reflection on the Christian Life.* New York: Doubleday, 1982.

Mechthild of Magdeburg. *The Flowing Light of the Godhead* in *The Classics of Western Spirituality.* Trans. Frank Tobin. New York: Paulist Press, 1998.

Meister Eckhart. *From Whom God Hid Nothing: Sermons, Writings, and Sayings.* Ed. David O'Neal. Boston, Mass.: Shambhala, 1996.

Meister Eckhart. The Essential Sermons, Commentaries, Treatises, and Defense in *The Classics of Western Spirituality.* New York: Paulist Press, 1981.

Meister Eckhart: Teacher and Preacher in *The Classics of Western Spirituality.* Ed. Bernard McGinn. New York: Paulist Press, 1981.

Merton, Thomas. *Contemplative Prayer.* New York: Herder and Herder, 1969.

__. *Seeds of Contemplation.* New York: Dell Publishing Co., 1957.

__. *Thoughts in Solitude.* New York: Garden City, N.Y.: Image Books, 1968.

__. *The Wisdom of the Desert: Sayings from the Desert Fathers of the Fourth Century.* London: Sheldon Press, 1974.

"Message and Meaning of the Ecumenical Council" in *The Documents of Vatican II.* Eds. Walter M. Abbot and Joseph Gallagher. New York: The America Press, 1966.

Muto, Susan. *Approaching the Sacred: An Introduction to Spiritual Reading.* Denville, N.J.: Dimension Books, 1973.

__. *Blessings that Make Us Be: A Formative Approach to Living the Beatitudes.* Petersham, Mass.: St. Bede's, 1982.

__. *Celebrating the Single Life: A Spirituality for Single Persons in Today's World.* New York: Crossroad, 1989.

__. *Dear Master: Letters on Spiritual Direction Inspired by Saint John of the Cross.* Liguori, Mo.: Liguori Publications, 1999.

__. *John of the Cross for Today: The Ascent.* Pittsburgh, Pa.: Epiphany Books, 1998.

__. *John of the Cross for Today: The Dark Night.* Pittsburgh, Pa.: Epiphany Books, 2000.

__. *The Journey Homeward: On the Road of Spiritual Reading.* Denville, N.J.: Dimension Books, 1977.

__. *Pathways of Spiritual Living.* Petersham, Mass.: St. Bede's Publications, 1988.

__. *A Practical Guide to Spiritual Reading.* Petersham, Mass.: St. Bede's Publications, 1994.

__. *Steps Along the Way: The Path of Spiritual Reading.* Denville, N.J.: Dimension Books, 1975.

__. *The Woman's Guide to the Catechism of the Catholic Church.* Ann Arbor, Mich.: Servant, 1997.

__. *Words of Wisdom for Our World: The Precautions and Counsels of St. John of the Cross.* Washington, D.C.: Institute of Carmelite Studies, 1995.

___and Adrian van Kaam. *Commitment: Key to Christian Maturity.* New York: Paulist Press, 1989.

__ and Adrian van Kaam. *Commitment: Key to Christian Maturity: A Workbook and Study Guide.* New York: Paulist Press, 1991.

__ and Adrian van Kaam. *Divine Guidance: Seeking to Find and Follow the Will of God.* Pittsburgh, Pa.: Epiphany Books, 2000.

New American Bible. Fireside Edition. Wichita, Kans.: Catholic Bible Publishers, 1992-1993.

New Dictionary of Catholic Spirituality. Ed. Michael Downey. Collegeville, Minn.: Liturgical Press, 1993.

Newman Today. Volume I. The Proceedings of the Wethersfield Institute. San Francisco: Ignatius Press, 1988.

Nicholas of Cusa: Selected Spiritual Writings in *The Classics of Western Spirituality*. Trans. H. Lawrence Bond. New York: Paulist Press, 1997.

Nouwen, Henri J. M. *The Return of the Prodigal Son: A Story of Homecoming*. Garden City, N.Y.: Image Books, 1994.

__. *Seeds of Hope*. Ed. Robert Durback. Garden City, N.Y.: Image Books, 1997.

Origen. *An Exhortation to Martyrdom* in *The Classics of Western Spirituality*. Trans. Rowan A. Greer. New York: Paulist Press, 1979.

Otto, Rudolph. *Mysticism East and West*. Wheaton, Ill.: Theophysical Publishing House, 1987.

Pennington, M. Basil. *Centering Prayer: Renewing an Ancient Christian Prayer Form*. Garden City, N.Y.: Image Books, 1980.

Perspectives on Charismatic Renewal. Ed. Edward D. O'Connor. Notre Dame, Ind.: University of Notre Dame Press, 1975.

The Philokalia, Volume One. Trans. G. E. H. Palmer, Philip Sherrard, and Kallistos Ware. London: Faber and Faber, 1979.

The Philokalia, Volume Two. Trans. G. E. H. Palmer, Philip Sherrard, and Kallistos Ware. London: Faber and Faber, 1981.

The Philokalia, Volume Three. Trans. G. E. H. Palmer, Philip Sherrard, and Kallistos Ware. London: Faber and Faber, 1984.

The Philokalia, Volume Four. Trans. G. E. H. Palmer, Philip Sherrard, and Kallistos Ware. London: Faber and Faber, 1995.

The Pilgrim's Tale in *The Classics of Western Spirituality*. Trans. T. Allen Smith. New York: Paulist Press, 1999.

The Prayers of Catherine of Siena. Ed. Suzanne Noffke. New York: Paulist Press, 1983.

The Prayers and Meditations of St. Anselm. Trans. Sister Benedicta Ward. New York: Penguin Books, 1973.

Pseudo-Dionysius. *The Complete Works* in *The Classics of Western Spirituality.* Trans. Colm Luibheid. New York: Paulist Press, 1987.

Richard of St. Victor. *The Twelve Patriarchs, The Mystical Ark, Book Three of the Trinity* in *The Classics of Western Spirituality.* Trans. Grover A. Zinn. New York: Paulist Press, 1979.

Rolle, Richard. *The English Writings* in *The Classics of Western Spirituality.* Trans. Rosamund S. Allen. New York: Paulist Press, 1988.

The Rule of St. Benedict. Ed. Timothy Fry. Collegeville, Minn.: The Liturgical Press, 1981.

Seraphim of Sarov. *Little Russian Philokalia.* Volume I:. New Valaam Monastery, Alaska, St. Herman Press, 1991.

The Sayings of the Desert Fathers: The Alphabetical Collection. Trans. Sister Benedicta Ward. Kalamazoo, Mich.: Cistercian Publications, 1975.

Seton, Elizabeth Ann St. *Selected Writings* in *Sources of American Spirituality.* Ed. Ellin Kelly and Annabelle Melville. New York: Paulist Press, 1987.

Spidlik, Thomas. *Drinking from the Hidden Fountain: A Patristic Breviary.* Trans. Paul Drake. Kalamazoo, Mich.: Cistercian Publications, 1994.

Stein, Edith. *Self Portrait in Letters 1916-1942* in *The Collected Works,* Volume 1. Trans. Kieran Kavanaugh and Otilio Rodriquez. Washington, D.C.: Institute of Carmelite Studies, 1976.

Suso, Blessed Henry. *The Exemplar with Two German Sermons* in *The Classics of Western Spirituality.* Trans. Frank Tobin. New York: Paulist Press, 1989.

Symeon the New Theologian. *Hymns of Divine Love.* Trans. George A. Maloney. Denville, N.Y.: Dimension Books, n.d.

___. *The Discourses* in *The Classics of Western Spirituality.* Trans. C. J. De Catanzaro. New York: Paulist Press, 1980.

Tauler, John. *Sermons* in *The Classics of Western Spirituality.* Trans. Maria Shrady. New York: Paulist Press, 1985.

Thérèse of Lisieux, St. *Story of a Soul: The Autobiography of St. Thérèse of Lisieux.* Trans. John Clarke. Washington, D.C.: Institute of Carmelite Studies, 1976.

___. *Poetry.* Trans. Donald Kinney, O.C.D. Washington, D.C.: Institute of Carmelite Studies, 1996.

Tetlow, Joseph A. *Ignatius Loyola: Spiritual Exercises.* New York: Crossroad, 1996.

Underhill, Evelyn. *Mysticism.* New York: Dutton, 1961.

Van Kaam, Adrian. *Formation of the Human Heart.* Formative Spirituality Series. Volume Three. New York: Crossroad/Continuum, 1986.

___. *Looking for Jesus.* Denville, N.J.: Dimension Books, 1978.

___. *The Dynamics of Spiritual Self-Direction.* Pittsburgh, Pa.: Epiphany Books, 2000.

___. *The Vowed Life.* Denville, N.J.: Dimension Books, 1968.

__ and Susan Muto. *Practicing the Prayer of Presence.* Williston Park, N.Y.: Resurrection Press, 1993.

Vincent de Paul, St. and Louise de Marillac, St. *Rules, Conferences, and Writings* in *The Classics of Western Spirituality.* Ed. Frances Ryan and John Rybolt. New York: Paulist Press, 1995.

The Works of St. Cyril of Jerusalem in *The Fathers of the Church.* Volume One. Trans. Leo. P. McCauley. Washington, D.C.: The Catholic University of America Press, 1969.

Welch, John. *The Carmelite Way: An Ancient Path for Today's Pilgrim.* New York: Paulist Press, 1996.

Western Asceticism in *The Library of Christian Classics: Ichthus Edition.* Edited by Owen Chadwick. Philadelphia, Pa.: Westminster Press, n.d.

Westminster Dictionary of Christian Spirituality. Ed. Gordon S. Wakefield. Philadelphia, Pa.: Westminster Press, 1983.

William of St. Thierry. *The Golden Epistle: A Letter to the Brethren at Mont Dieu* in *Cistercian Fathers Series,* Number Twelve. Trans. Theodore Berkeley. Spencer, Mass.: Cistercian Publications, 1971.

Wright, Wendy M. *Francis De Sales: Introduction to the Devout Life and Treatise on the Love of God.* New York: Crossroad, 1993.

About the Author

Susan Muto, Ph.D., executive director of the Epiphany Association and a native of Pittsburgh, is a renowned speaker, author, and teacher. A single lay woman living her vocation in the world and doing full-time church-related ministry in the Epiphany Association, she has led conferences, seminars, workshops, and institutes throughout the world.

Professor Muto received her Ph.D. in English literature from the University of Pittsburgh, where she specialized in the work of post-Reformation spiritual writers. Beginning in 1966, she served in various administrative positions at the Institute of Formative Spirituality (IFS) at Duquesne University and taught as a full professor in its programs, edited its journals, and served as its director from 1981 to 1988. An expert in literature and spirituality, she continues to teach courses on an adjunct basis at many schools, seminaries, and centers of higher learning. She aims in her teaching to integrate the life of prayer and presence with professional ministry and in-depth formation in the home, the church, and the marketplace. In faithfulness to the principles of the original European Epiphany approach, she addresses her teachings to the contemporary needs of laity, clergy, and religious.

As coeditor of *Epiphany Connexions* and *Epiphany International*, as a frequent contributor to scholarly and popular journals, and as herself the author and coauthor of over thirty books, Dr. Muto keeps up to date with the latest developments in her field. In fact, her many books on formative reading of Scripture and the masters are considered to be premier introductions to the basic, classical art and discipline of spiritual formation and its systematic, comprehensive formation theology. She lectures nationally and internationally on the treasured wisdom of the Judeo-Christian faith and formation tradition and on many foundational facets of living human and Christian values in today's world. Professor Muto holds memberships in numerous honorary organizations and has received many distinctions for her work, including a Doctor of Humanities degree from King's College in Wilkes-Barre, Pennsylvania.